Village W

—— in ——

ESSEX

Village Walks in ESSEX

Ann and Norman Skinner

COUNTRYSIDE BOOKS
NEWBURY, BERKSHIRE

COUNTRYSIDE BOOKS
3 Catherine Road
Newbury, Berkshire

ISBN 1 85306 514 5

Designed by Graham Whiteman
Photographs and maps by the authors
Illustrations by Trevor Yorke

Produced through MRM Associates Ltd., Reading
Printed by Woolnough Bookbinding Ltd., Irthlingborough

Contents

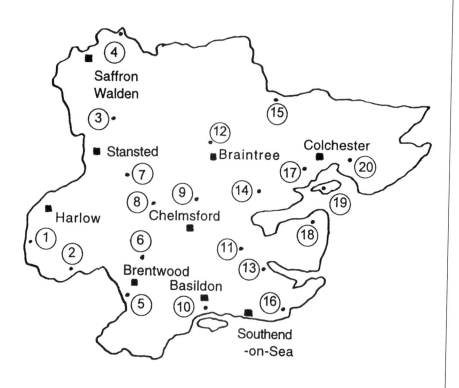

AREA MAP SHOWING LOCATIONS OF THE WALKS.

④ Saffron Walden

③

⑮

⑫

Stansted ■
Braintree ■
Colchester ■

⑦

⑰
⑳

⑧ ⑨
⑭

Chelmsford
⑲

Harlow ■
⑥

① ② ⑪
⑱

Brentwood ⑬
Basildon ■

⑤ ⑩ ⑯
Southend -on-Sea

WALK

Publisher's Note

We hope that you obtain considerable enjoyment from this book; great care has been taken in its preparation. Although at the time of publication all routes followed public rights of way or permitted paths, diversion orders can be made and permissions withdrawn.

We cannot of course be held responsible for such diversion orders and any inaccuracies in the text which result from these or any other changes to the routes nor any damage which might result from walkers trespassing on private property. We are anxious though that all details covering the walks are kept up to date and would therefore welcome information from readers which would be relevant to future editions.

Introduction

Essex, as the Tourist Board tells us, is a county full of hidden treasures. This clever advertising slogan does in fact describe rather well the rich tapestry of history, architecture and tradition that, put with different soil types, rivers, woods, coastline and hills, makes this such an exciting county both to live and walk in.

In this book of village walks, we have tried to include as many different parts of the county as possible so there should be at least one walk quite near to where you live. In the north we have the hilly village of Hadstock and both beauty and history in Wormingford. In Henham we find the traditional, with the ducks on the pond, alongside the modern farming ventures of llamas and ostriches. Gosfield with its large boating lake and Sandpits nature reserve adds contrast again. Great Bardfield has a fine collection of old buildings beautifully grouped so you can just spend a while looking from one picture postcard scene to another. Layer de la Haye, by contrast, has more a sprinkling of properties lining the road over several miles, many having superb views over the reservoir. The walk from Wivenhoe, like Great Wakering, is for us at its best on a sunny day when the tide is in, but bird watchers will probably prefer to be there at low tide to spot the wading birds.

Lambourne End takes one deep into Hainault Forest; how wonderful to find this so close to London. Ingatestone's taste of history with its fine Hall, combined with some superb views from Buttsbury, make this area a very interesting place both to visit and live and work in. Great Warley must give Ford's German visitors a chance to learn Essex is far from flat! We are still surprised what a number of hills there are on a walk round this village. In Great Saling we get the connection with *Lovejoy*, especially as we visit his local at the end of the walk. The walks from West Mersea and Bradwell give wide views of each other; what fun it is to pick out places you have been, one from the other. One could go on. Waltham Abbey, Little Waltham, Fobbing, East Hanningfield, Battlesbridge and Great Braxted all have much to offer whether in the way of history, views or interest to bird lovers. You will find at times isolation where you expect houses, bustle and antiques when perhaps a rundown mill may well have been more likely. What we do hope is that you will get as much fun from visiting our villages in Essex as we have done.

The sketch maps provided in the book are designed to guide you round the route but they are not drawn to scale. We strongly recommend that when preparing for your visit you take with you the Ordnance Survey map for the area. Pathfinder or Explorer maps may be of even more assistance than the Landranger ones mentioned in the text. Whilst appreciating they are extremely expensive to buy it may be possible to borrow one from the library. If you have a compass take this along also, it is a very useful aid on days when the sun does not come out and it would help you to be sure of the direction in which you are walking. Regular walkers will not need us to tell them to take a waterproof on days it may rain, hats and gloves on cold days, and sun hats on warm days.

It is nice to have a small bottle of water or fruit drink with you, on summer days especially, to quench the thirst. Children like to have the occasional sweet to keep up their strength so take some if they are members of your party. If a suitable refreshment place has come to our notice we have included details of this for you. Some of the walks go past wonderful picnic spots and we have suggested places we liked. Included also are details of pubs we have visited and some of the many meals we enjoyed whilst preparing this book. Sometimes it is an advantage if you ring and book a table in advance, or to check the opening hours.

To make your day out even more enjoyable, places of interest nearby have been noted in a special section within each walk. Many villages do not have a village car park so we have chosen places where a car or two should be able to be left for a few hours without causing any problems. Please make sure you are not blocking a drive or parking somewhere unsuitable. If you do want to park in the pub car park for any reason, please ask the landlord first.

We would both like to thank local footpath secretaries who have given advice on some less familiar paths, and family and friends who have encouraged us in this venture.

We have each chosen our more favoured villages to write about. They have all been visited, and the walks walked out jointly. We have practised the discussions that come from missing a path and know the frustration of having to retrace one's steps. Many of the paths are well walked, with most now having good waymarks. It is always, we find, when you come to the tricky bit there is no indication or the path has just been ploughed out! We have tried to make the way doubly clear in these circumstances in the text.

We do hope with the use of this book you will be finding your way to new locations and enjoying new walks from the lovely villages of Essex.

Ann and Norman Skinner

WALTHAM ABBEY

Length: 4¾ miles

Getting there: From junction 26 on the M11 take the A121 signed Waltham Abbey. At the town centre keep on the A121, do not turn left down Sun Street. The Lee Valley Countryside Centre is clearly signed; you take the first exit at the next	roundabout to get into the pay car park. **Parking:** The car park charges 50p for up to 4 hours; this gives plenty of time to do the walk and have a bite to eat. Free car parking is available where WC	❹ is shown on the map. This can be entered at the turning past the River Lee Navigation. **Map:** OS Landranger – Luton and Hertford 166 (GR 384008).

Waltham Abbey village is a delightful cluster of buildings round the area of the Abbey church. It lies on the Greenwich Meridian 0 degree longitude, which you cross as you begin the walk.

An abbey has stood on this site since King Harold built the first in 1060. He is reputed to be buried in the Abbey grounds. Henry II founded the Augustinian Abbey here in 1177. Over the centuries many people have found inspiration in this lovely setting. Tennyson wrote of the bells of Waltham Abbey, and Thomas Tallis, organist until the Abbey was dissolved in 1540, was a notable musician. He provided the setting for the words of the Anglican service. You can find out more about the history of the area at the museum situated in Sun Street in two timber-framed houses dating from 1520 and 1760.

The nearby Lee Navigation, once used in the transport of gunpowder for the arms factory, is now a delightful place where fishermen, walkers and cyclists rub shoulders with narrow-boat visitors. Leaving the village behind, you walk along its bank as far as Waltham Common Lock, then turn north-east to visit Hall Marsh and Hooks Marsh Lakes. This is a rare treat for those interested in bird watching as there are hides nearby (bookable in advance) if you would like to try spotting snipe, teal, plover and bitterns.

At Fishers Green Lane a walk over open fields and a beautiful green track brings you back to the park to walk by Cornmill Stream and the Dragonfly Sanctuary. A tunnel under the A121 returns you to the Abbey grounds where one can wander for hours exploring the ruins and the beautiful rose gardens. A visit to the information centre is also a must so you can pick up leaflets to arrange your next visit to this interesting area!

THE WALK

❶ From the car park walk over to the information centre, passing the ruins of the old forge and crossing the Greenwich Meridian line on your way. From the centre take the black and white path to Waltham Abbey cloister. You enter the grounds under a brick doorway arch. Cross the Abbey Gardens and walk round with the Abbey on your right to pass a small oak tree planted in September 1997 in memory of Diana Princess of Wales.

❷ On leaving the Abbey pass the tourist office in Highbridge Street. I suggest you cross with the roundabout on your right, then cross back over the A121 on the pedestrian crossing.

❸ Continue ahead and take the footpath on your right opposite The Old English Gentleman pub. Go down the ramp to the canal side. You soon join a gravel path up to Waltham Town Lock.

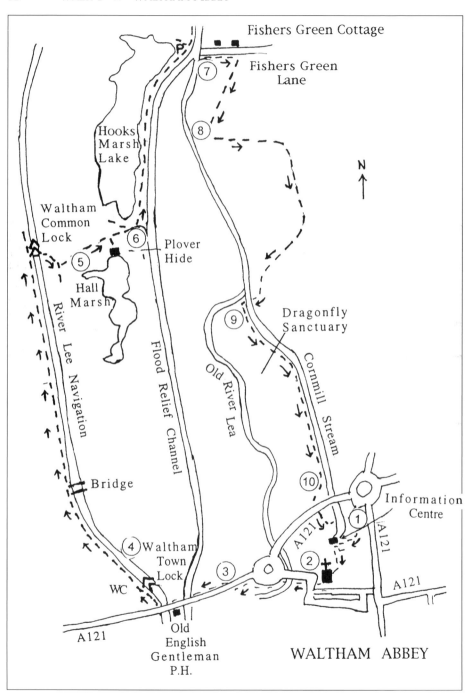

The River Lee Navigation.

❹ Continue along the canal to go under the bridge ahead. This stretch often has swans, dragonflies and canal boats. When you come to Waltham Common Lock, turn right and cross the concrete foot-bridge. Turn almost back on yourself, but now on the other side of the canal, passing a seat then crossing two excellent wooden bridges to enter Hall Marsh. Ignore the path to your right.

❺ You soon pass Plover Hide, which is kept locked. Go under the power lines and pass the old pill box to a junction of paths.

❻ Turn left up the cycle track. The Flood Relief Channel you are walking beside

later bears right past a five-bar gate and footpath sign. Just past this you come to Fishers Green Lane Car Park and sluice bridge.

❼ Cross the stream and go uphill, passing Fishers Green Farm. Opposite Fishers Green Cottage turn right over a stile by a footpath sign. A barbed wire fence is on your right.

❽ Partway across this field you come to a sign for Cornmill Meadows. Turn left here and head slightly uphill across the field till you come to a high wire fence with con-crete posts. Another sign to Cornmill Meadows points the way over a crossing track, and through a kissing gate back into

Waltham Town Lock.

the park. Follow the fence right and then left till you come to a bridge over Cornmill Stream to enter the Dragonfly Sanctuary.

❾ Turn left to walk with the stream on your left. Go through a kissing gate and over an earth bridge.

❿ Bear rightish towards a kissing gate, turn right and left to go through a tunnel under the road. A gravel path ahead takes you over the river. Turn left down three steps and go through the metal gate. Continue ahead to a second metal gate. Now head half-right back to your car. A detour just a little further right will enable you to visit the Rose Garden.

LAMBOURNE END

Length: 3¾ miles

Getting there: From the north-east of the county, drive through Ongar and take the A113 through Stanford Rivers. At Passingford Bridge exit the roundabout on the B175 towards Stapleford Abbotts. Before getting there turn off right and right again at a T junction. Soon turn left signposted to Lambourne, and coming to the Camelot turn left into the Forest car park. From the south of the county go north along Straight Road, off Gallows Corner. At the road junction turn right and very soon left to Havering Atte Bower. Follow this road (B175) through the village and down-hill. After a left-hand corner follow the signs to Abridge on the left, and again left to Lambourne and the Camelot. Access is easy from West Essex and East London. Join the B173 through Chigwell Row to the Camelot, turning right off the road into the car park.

Parking: There is good parking opposite the Camelot. You could also park near Lambourne church and follow the walk from there.

Map: OS Landranger – East London 177 or Chelmsford and Harlow 167 (GR 478944 Camelot or 479961 church).

This parish stands high above the river Roding and is on surprisingly hilly ground, always an attraction when it occurs in Essex. The village is split into three little centres of population. Firstly in the south, just beyond Hainault Forest, are some houses grouped around the Camelot pub. Little more than ½ mile to the north is Lambourne End, not far from Bishops Hall, and a further ¾ mile north sit Lambourne church and Lambourne Hall in a glorious position with panoramic views. Parts of the church are of Norman origin, notably the two doorways, and the Hall was built in Elizabethan times.

From the edge of Hainault Forest this delightful walk heads north to Lambourne End village and onwards to the church, where time may be spent admiring the exterior (sometimes the church is open, for closer inspection inside). There is a good view towards London Docklands to enjoy. You travel back south on a bridleway through Gallmans End Farm into the forest. Finally you traverse west through the forest and north back to the car park, along broad grassy tracks.

THE WALK

❶ Cross the road to the Camelot and follow the road just to its right. Soon pass

---

FOOD and DRINK

The Camelot is a Beefeater pub and is well able to cater for your requirements. Telephone: 0181 500 7712. However, it can be fairly busy at times. In these circumstances you may wish to go slightly further afield to the pubs in Abridge or Stapleford Abbotts.

Hop Pole Farm on the left, a reminder that hops were once an extensive crop in Essex. You come to a concrete footpath sign curiously marked 'In field'.

❷ Turn right over the stile and walk uphill in a pasture field to another stile, past a little pond. Look back here to the south-west to Canary Wharf in London. Then continue uphill to a stile on your left, leading on to a road at the village. Turn right at a concrete footpath sign and follow the road.

❸ Just beyond the last house in the village turn left at another concrete footpath sign. Follow the fence on the left to a kissing gate into a pasture field. Walk with the hedge to your right. Pass a pond and continue aiming for Lambourne church, to cross a stile into an arable field. Follow the path down to the church with a hedge to your right. At the field corner go through the kissing gate under a glorious Scots pine and an oak.

❹ Turn right (ignoring an arrow pointing left) to the church, pausing perhaps to admire the church and to look in if it is open.

❺ Further on at a corner turn right uphill following a sign marked Abridge Country Walk. Soon take a bridleway to Lambourne End through Conduit Wood, with a fence on the left and a hedge on the right. Further, pass Gallmans End Farm out of the wood. The path now follows with a hedge on the left, a fence on the right out on to the farmstead.

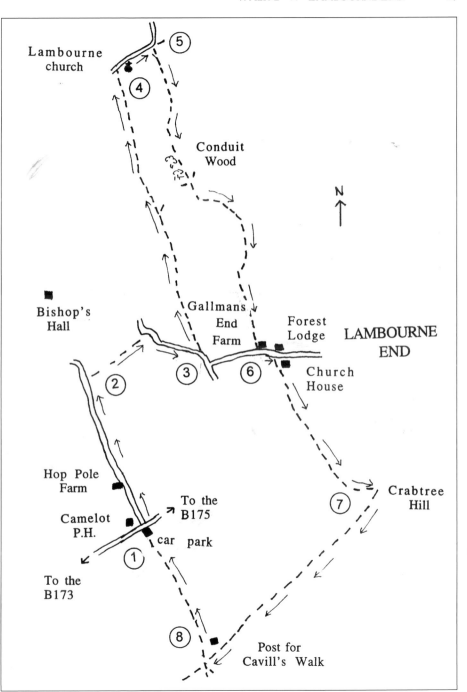

A kissing gate, with Lambourne church in the background.

❻ On reaching the road turn left past a house and Forest Lodge. At a corner, turn right at a concrete footpath sign under a willow tree at Church House, onto a grassy lane and over a waymarked stile.

❼ The path after Crabtree Hill follows two separate yellow arrows on to a broad track, turning right on a long uphill section to the south of the wood.

❽ At a post commemorating Cavill's Walk turn right, heading north on an even broader track back to the car park.

HENHAM

Length: 4½ miles

Getting there: If coming from central or east Essex it is better to be on the A120 west of Great Dunmow. At the traffic lights in Takeley turn right and then left at Bambers Green past Molehill Green towards Elsenham. Turn right along the B1051 and after about ¾ mile turn left to Henham. Those coming from the west of the county may prefer to use the M11, leaving at junction 8 and proceeding to Stansted Mountfitchet. Turn right towards the station and join the B1051 through Elsenham turning off left at the Henham sign.

Parking: The walk starts from the vicinity of the church so when the church is not in use it should be all right to park there. At other times park on the High Street taking care not to obstruct driveways etc.

Map: OS Landranger – Chelmsford and Harlow 167 (GR 545285).

The major features of Henham, which make the village so attractive, are the wide greens alongside its streets and the many ponds along the High Street. Amongst pretty cottages with their long gardens there is much half timbering and thatch. Henham is a 'picture' village and truly a delightful place.

At a bend in the road the church stands well back. It dates mainly from the 13th century, with a neat 'Hertfordshire spike' as a spire, and is well worth a visit.

In 1669 the village was said to be plagued by a sensational 'winged serpent' some nine feet long. It proved impossible to catch and eventually disappeared of its own accord, though not before it had brought fame to Henham. Even a public house in Covent Garden was named the Essex Serpent after the story was published.

This enjoyable walk passes through the village, then on a direct field path to Lovecotes Farm. You walk along a shaded green lane to Amberden Hall. From the Hall the route follows a glorious rolling path to Henham Lodge and thence back to Henham, the pub and the church. Enjoy the contrast between the ducks on the village ponds and the ostriches being farmed nearby!

THE WALK

❶ From where you park your car, near the church or in the High Street, walk to the east along the High Street. First you will pass the Post Office Stores and in the gardens on your left there are several large ponds, sometimes with ducks. The High Street becomes Chickney Road.

❷ After a right-hand bend turn left off the road by a concrete public footpath sign and walk on a straight path through crops. Pass a sports field over to your right. Ahead on the left is a large transmission tower. After about ½ mile on the field path you return to the road and continue past Lovecotes Farm.

❸ Turn left at a concrete public bridleway sign, soon passing close by the transmission tower. The green lane you are on is an old road from years ago. Between two power lines turn sharply to the right to a junction with another bridleway.

❹ Turn left along the lane.

❺ Look for a black public footpath sign and turn left along a concrete drive to the farm steading beside Amberden Hall. Continue in the same direction through the steading and into open country. This is a glorious route. Pass over a ditch at the hedge end and follow the path through a crop division, going uphill. Now follow the track on the right to Henham Lodge. The track leads through a steading. Note

Ostriches at Henham Lodge.

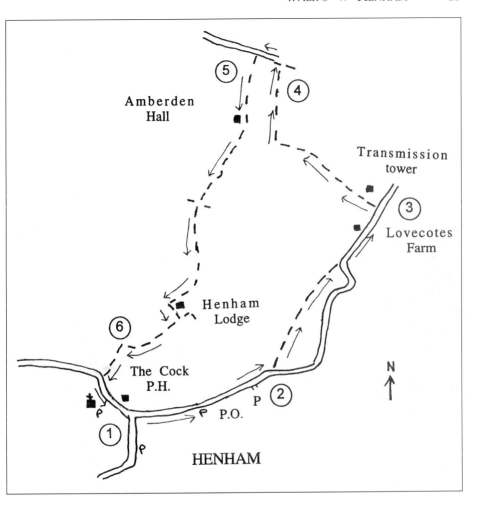

the weathervane with the white bull. There are several arrows waymarking the route but they all point in the opposite direction! Nevertheless, you *can* follow them against the flow. Turn left towards metal gates. Then turn right at some old fuel pumps. At this point there are ostriches and llamas in the field. These provide meat for the restaurant kitchen. Follow the track downhill to a path crossway.

❻ Turn left, still on the track, up to the pub and church of Henham.

HADSTOCK

Length: 5 miles

Getting there: From Saffron Walden drive north by the B1052 through Little Walden to Hadstock, a distance of about 4 miles.	Parking: At the centre of the village by the village green turn sharp right towards the church and follow the sign to the church parking.	Map: OS Landranger – Cambridge and Newmarket 154 (GR 562447).

Hadstock is the most northerly village in Essex, less than a mile from the border on the Linton road. Nestling amongst little hills, the village is watched over by the church which attracts visitors from afar. The church door has been in place since 1016. Other doors in the church include one 700 years old and two 600 years old.

In early medieval times Hadstock was an important place with a weekly market on Wednesdays, and an annual fair on St Botolph's Day. Look out for the water pump by the village green made by Chas Lock & Sons Ltd Engineers, Cottenham, Cambridgeshire. The pump is operated by a wheel and handle.

FOOD and DRINK

In such a tiny village the job of providing food and drink falls to the sole pub, the King's Head, a 300 year old local. There are usually four real ales which rotate from a larger list. This includes a mild as well as many famous bitters. Food can be chosen from a selection on the blackboard – we found great satisfaction from the tasty meals we chose. The pub has three fine brick fireplaces, and a small area with a three-piece suite and a piano especially for those who enjoy the sensation of drinking at home! Food is served on six days, Monday to Saturday. There is no food on Sundays, so hungry walkers may look slightly further afield in Linton. Telephone: 01223 893473.

Views over the surrounding countryside greet you as you leave Hadstock on this lovely walk. The route takes you past the remains of an old windmill and along the banks of the river Granta to Linton, with its pretty houses and ford populated by ducks. You return to Hadstock along part of the Icknield Way.

THE WALK
❶ Walk back downhill from the car park to the village green.

❷ Turn right uphill for 175 yards. Turn left at a concrete footpath sign into Manley Lane. When you come to Briar Cottage, a thatched building at the end of the lane, enter a sports field, crossing this to the far left corner. The path continues across an arable field to the facing hedge. This is the summit of Haws Hill, not so high but commanding all-round views of the countryside.

❸ Bear right along the field edge with a

hedge on your right, downhill, for the length of the field.

❹ At the corner turn right onto a track and left with the track over an old railway bridge. Pass Windmill House, with the base of the old windmill behind. About 200 yards past Malting Cottages look for a stile and a waymark in the right-hand hedge.

❺ Here cross the field to the road and continue over towards the hedge corner.

❻ Bear left to join the bank of the river Granta. Do not cross the first bridge but carry on along the bank to turn right over the second bridge.

❼ Soon pass the church at Linton and turn left to the church gate. Pass some lovely old houses, recrossing the river on a bridge by a ford full of ducks. The road (Ham Lane) crosses the High Street into Market Street which you follow. Pass to the left of Dovedale Close to reach a large sports ground.

❽ Turn left along the boundary of a cricket pitch, bearing right by a bowling green. Leave the sports field at waymarks. Do not cross the stile on the left but follow a broad grassy path between temporary fences.

❾ When you reach buildings at Little Linton Farm, exit at kissing gates. Turn left on the bridleway and follow this lane to the A604. Cross with care. You are on the Icknield Way. Walk through some new farm developments onto a track which

A charming old house near Linton church.

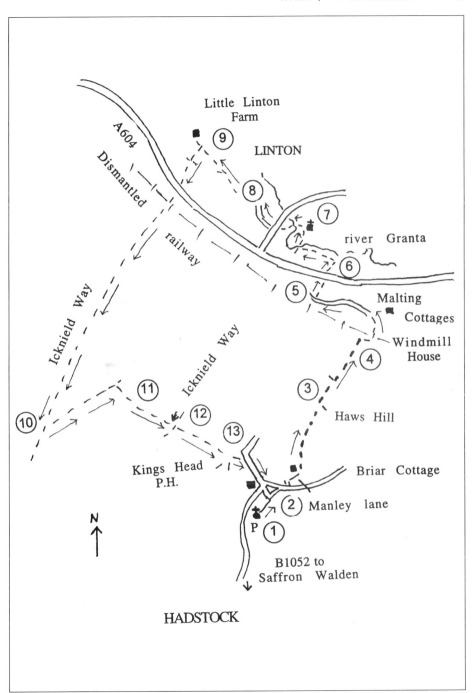

Little Linton Farm

LINTON

A604

Dismantled

railway

Icknield Way

Icknield Way

river Granta

Malting Cottages

Windmill House

Haws Hill

Kings Head P.H.

Briar Cottage

Manley lane

P

B1052 to Saffron Walden

N

HADSTOCK

slowly climbs to the ridge ahead.

⑩ After just over a mile from the road, trees begin to line the track. Here turn left back on yourself to face north-east, aiming for a small clump of trees across the valley.

Pass waymarks on the way and just after going under some power lines turn right to a hedge gap.

⑪ Through the hedge continue on a field edge to a facing hedge.

⑫ Take care here. Ignore an Icknield Way sign to the right. Turn left for a few yards to locate a waymark pointing over a double plank bridge through a hedge. Now you go straight on past a short section of hedge. Shortly a coal yard emerges on the right. Pass this and turn left through a gate to reach the roadside.

⑬ Turn right and walk back to the village.

WALK 5

GREAT WARLEY

Length: 5¾ miles

Getting there: From the A127, near the M25 interchange, turn onto the B186 uphill for just over a mile into the centre of Great Warley village. Turn left in the middle of the village. After 300 yards turn left into Bere-dens Lane. This is now a dead end and there is usually parking for one or two cars at the bottom.

Parking: As described above, parking is available in Beredens Lane. At a different part of the walking route it is sometimes possible to park outside Great Warley church, and there is a car park off Nags Head Lane in Tylers Common which is close to the route.

Map: OS Landranger – East London area 177 (GR 578899).

The M25 is not far away but Great Warley has not lost its charm. The centre of the village lies on a hilltop, with magnificent panoramic views to be enjoyed. Woodland fills the foreground as you take time to get your bearings. Round the green on this hilltop stand old buildings and a 15th century public house, reputedly haunted! The church of St Mary, which lies half-way down the hill, was built as a memorial to his brother by the lord of the manor, Mr Evelyn Heseltine in 1902. It is an unusual parish church, designed in contemporary Art Nouveau style, and well worth a visit.

This is an exhilarating walk, soon bringing you to a viewpoint looking over to the Langdon Hills. Woods and farm land provide the backdrop as you walk towards Great Warley village centre and church, before circling round to cross the

M25. From Tylers Common a lovely lane brings you back to the start.

THE WALK
❶ From Beredens Lane cross the stile by the footpath direction post. Immediately turn left with a hedge on your left up a grass track. At the top of the field turn right by the wood side, follow this round. From this field there are magnificent views to the right of Langdon Hills.

❷ The path moves a few yards away from the woods and you follow by a yellow arrow, turning left along with a hedge on your right to reach a farm road.

❸ Turn right through the farm steading at

Great Warley church.

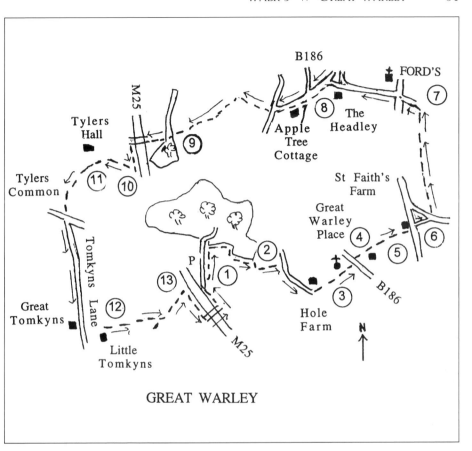

GREAT WARLEY

Hole Farm. Now turn left pass the timbered farmhouse. Cross a little field and join a steep track. Carry on with this track to the road where you turn left to Great Warley church.

❹ Cross over the road with care and over a stile, passing Great Warley Place. At the field corner cross another stile. Head slightly left and downhill to an arrowed signpost.

❺ Cross over a bridge with a stile before and after, and walk steeply uphill with a hedge on the left to St Faith's Farm. Here there is a gate to be opened, taking care not to allow ponies to escape. Walk through the exercise ring to reach the road.

❻ Turn left and very soon right along Magpie Lane. At the end of the little green, cross the road and follow the path signposted to Warley Gap. There are fairly good waymarks in this wood and soon we reach Ford's offices at Warley.

❼ Turn left and cross the road in the same

PLACES of INTEREST

To the east is the **Thorndon Country Park**, Countryside Centre run jointly with the Essex Wildlife Trust. Open daily (telephone: 01277 211250). At South Weald to the north is the **Weald Country Park**, once an estate with a medieval deer park. Also open daily (telephone: 01277 261343). Both have visitor centres, exhibitions and refreshments.

---

direction to follow the lane to the Headley. Past the Headley turn left along a narrow path.

❽ Cross the busy road on the right at Great Ropers Lane and continue along a wide track past Apple Tree Cottage. At the road turn left and then right along a fenced path. Crossing a stile into a field, keep to the fence on the right and after a left turn cross a stile on your right and follow the hedge on the left.

❾ Pass through a gate into a wood and continue straight on over the bridge crossing the M25. Turn left downhill.

❿ At the bottom cross a stile to walk back up the other side. Pass over a stile into Tylers Common and continue uphill towards a house (Tylers Hall).

⓫ Find a broad grass track leading left away from the house and follow this over the common to the road. Cross this road and walk down Tomkyns Lane. Continue up this lane for ½ mile.

⓬ Opposite Great Tomkyns and passing to the left of the side boundary of Little Tomkyns is a path. At present there is a disagreement as to whether it is a footpath or bridleway and so no direction post has been erected but you can be sure you have every right to use it. It is one of the finest paths in the area. After reaching the end of Little Tomkyns, continue over two stiles and through a paddock gate to an arrow pointing right near the motorway.

⓭ Cross one more stile downhill to the bridge. Cross over and by a narrow path reach the bottom of Beredens Lane.

INGATESTONE

Length: 5½ miles

Getting there: Approach Ingatestone by way of the A12. From the south, exit as indicated and drive through the village to the last road on the left – New Road. The car park is by the playing field on the right. From the north, the way goes through Margaretting and as soon as you reach Ingatestone turn right into New Road.

Parking: You may park as indicated above. If you prefer, there is a long stay car park at the rear of the Community Club car park which is 150 yards along the High Street to the south-west of New Road.

Map: OS Landranger – Chelmsford and Harlow 167 (GR 651999).

Ingatestone is an attractive village much sought after as a residence by locals and commuters alike. Since the 1500s it has been the home of the Petre family. The first Lord Petre was a faithful follower of Henry VIII and the line of succession has continued to the present day. The church dates from the 15th century and under the chancel and the chapel he built, Sir William Petre lies on his tomb with his wife, looking up at the coat of arms suspended above him. The Petres' home,

FOOD and DRINK

There are four pubs in Ingatestone. For eating purposes the pick is the Bell in the High Street (telephone: 01277 353314), while the character pub is the Star near the church (telephone: 01277 353618). There are also good Chinese and Indian restaurants. Above all is Little Hammonds, also in the High Street, where fine cuisine and wines may be enjoyed.

Ingatestone Hall with its many delightful stepped gables, has a pleasant look of Elizabethan days about it.

Even the tunnel under the A12 has a story to it on this varied walk. The tunnel was only built with the good graces of Ernest Marples, Minister of Transport when the Ingatestone bypass was built in the early Sixties. His response on the opening day to locals who complained of the lack of access from the north end of the village was to commit his department to building a tunnel. Such a cavalier attitude sadly does not happen today!

Quiet lanes, paths and woods bring you around towards Margaretting church, and then you head for another ancient church at Buttsbury, along by the river Wid. You will pass Ingatestone Hall on the return to the village.

THE WALK
❶ From the car park walk up New Road for 200 yards. At the end of the road a metal railed, concrete pathway on the right leads down into a tunnel which passes under the A12 trunk road.

❷ After negotiating the tunnel follow Little Hyde Lane for about 700 yards up

this quiet road. At the top Back Lane goes off to the left but you continue round a right angle still on Little Hyde Lane. Just past Grove Cottage turn left at a footpath post through bushes and trees.

❸ At the end of the wood cross a stile and immediately turn right on a path with a wood on your right. Cross another stile. When you reach a crossing hedge, cross a stile and turn right to a stile in a hedge. Cross this and turn left uphill with a hedge on your left, to a stile.

❹ Over the stile turn right down Dog Kennel Lane. As the lane turns right, turn left by a St Peter's Way signpost over a stile. Now turn right to another stile and go straight on to a further stile which takes you into a wood, Bushey Wood. Through the wood cross a plank bridge over the stream.

❺ Turn left to the field corner and cross another plank bridge by a waymark. Turn right with the hedge on your right. Follow the stream on the right for 450 yards to a plank bridge on your right and a stile into a meadow.

❻ At the end of the meadow, near the

PLACES of INTEREST

Ingatestone Hall passed on the walk is well worth a visit. This 16th century mansion, set in 11 acres of grounds, is open from the end of March to September, on Saturday, Sunday and Bank Holidays. During the long school holidays it is also open on Wednesday, Thursday and Friday. Telephone: 01277 353010.

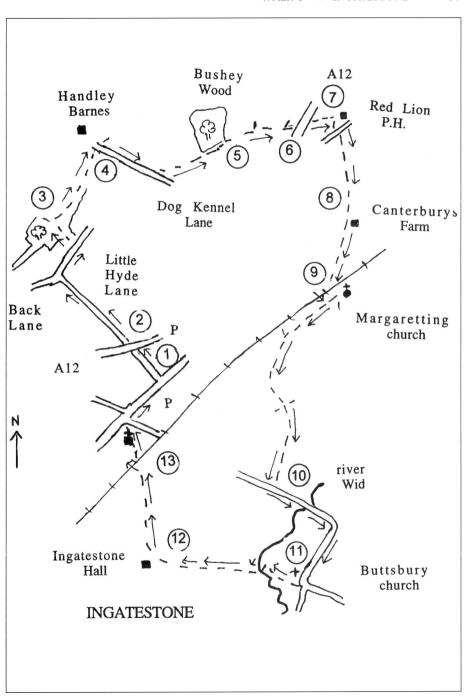

Buttsbury church.

elevated A12 trunk road, turn left and cross a stile. Now turn right through a large tunnel under the road to a stile at the side of a barn. Through the fenced pathway you reach a stile with a duck pond beside it, and continue to a gate.

❼ Through the gate turn right up to a stile and gate all in white, and a kissing gate which leads to the road. Cross over to another kissing gate by a concrete footpath post and follow the path to the far corner of the field. The path line basically follows the power lines above. At the corner at a gate and a stile cross into the next field, still following the lines now on your left.

❽ Cross another stile and go straight on with a fence on your right and a duck pond on your left to Canterbury's Farm. Cross over the farm track to a white gate. Walk on with a fence on your left over a plank bridge to a waymark post, and turn left towards the railway level crossing beside Margaretting church.

❾ Cross the railway lines and turn right, joining a permissive path which initially follows the railway lines for 500 yards before turning left down another concrete track. When you reach a junction of concrete tracks continue south, checking that the permissive footpath sign points that way! Now the track leads on to the Stock road, first crossing a stile.

❿ Turn left down the road to Buttsbury Bridge over the river Wid. Follow this road round a right bend to Buttsbury church.

⓫ Turn right immediately past the church and walk downhill to briefly follow the river Wid round to a bridge. Cross this and walk uphill to Ingatestone Hall, home of the Petre family.

⓬ Turn right at a footpath sign and cross a stile in the fence. Take a well defined path through the next field to a yellow arrow pointing across the railway bridge into Ingatestone playing field.

⓭ Cross the field towards the church tower. Reaching the church turn left to the High Street and right to the car park, be it Community Club car park or that in New Road.

GREAT BARDFIELD

Length: 4 miles

Getting there: From the western part of the county make for Great Dunmow and take the B1057 from Churchend to Great Bardfield. From the east take the B1053 from Braintree to Shalford village; turn left along a narrow road signposted to

Great Bardfield through Walthams Cross. From the south and through Chelmsford there is a quiet road by Felsted and Great Saling to Great Bardfield.

Parking: Below the road fork in

the High Street the road widens and easy parking is suggested there.

Map: OS Landranger – Chelmsford and Harlow 167 (GR 676306).

Great Bardfield was the favoured home of artists between the wars. The layout of the streets and the wonderfully varied houses and cottages make it a place of enormous charm. Once upon a time the village had its own market and a horse fair took place annually on the 22nd June.

The mannered simplicity of the formal facades has been borrowed from the city. A pleasant half hour stroll will reveal some of the delightful architecture of the place before heading from the centre to the parish church. This is richly decorated. The building has an obvious affinity with Stebbing church just over the hill. If they were not built by the same architect then they must have been influenced by each other.

Place House at the top of the High Street has an overhanging storey and a bracket carved to tell us it was built in 1564. The writer was grateful 20 years ago for the kindness of the owner who invited him to use the telephone when his car broke down outside. Apparently the ownership of the Place included the keys to two pews in the church which were known as 'Faculty' pews.

The village is the setting for some lovely walks. This one crosses the river Pant at a watermill and follows the Finchingfield Brook as far as the attractive house called Normans before climbing to a plateau affording views all round to Finchingfield church, Wethersfield and Great Bardfield windmill. The descent into the Pant valley and up to Walthams Cross precedes a lovely greenway leading to Great Bardfield church.

THE WALK

❶ The walk starts north towards the bridge over the river Pant. Before the bridge look for a gap in the houses on the right and follow a public footpath sign between them out to a field. Turn left and follow the field edge bending to the right.

❷ Go through a gap in the hedge and turn right along a marked path to a gate in front of an old red roofed cottage. Cross a stile into a steading. This is the old watermill which was alas burned down some years ago. Waymarks point to the right and left.

❸ Follow to the left over a brick bridge crossing the river Pant. Over a small field cross a metal bridge and immediately turn right along a field edge.

❹ At the field corner turn left with a tall hedge on your right. In 20 yards cross a stile with a waymark and continue through a meadow, soon veering right following the stream (Finchingfield Brook) over a stile and bridge to Normans, a very attractive house, part tiled, part thatched.

❺ Just adjacent to Normans cross a wooden bridge to the right over the brook. Climb up quite steeply by the hedge. There is a fine view of the windmill to your right. At the field corner step left through the ditch and then right (your original direction) across a wide arable field.

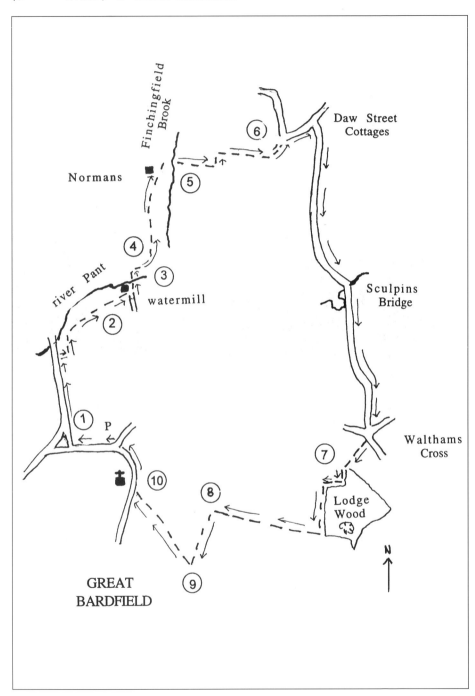

The watermill on the river Pant.

❻ At the end of the field turn onto a concrete farm track which soon comes to a road. Turn right and quite soon right again at Daw Street Cottages. This quiet country land leads south downhill through Daw Street to Sculpins Bridge over the river Pant. Now it is uphill for ½ mile to Walthams Cross. Cross straight over the road to an old footpath sign and a stile and a gate into a pasture field. Soon follow a yellow arrow out of the field and left through the wood.

❼ After a few yards turn right along the edge of the wood and follow the path, turning left on a path outside the wood to meet a crossing path by a hedge. Turn right and follow this path for ¾ mile.

❽ At another T junction turn left.

❾ Just after a large oak tree turn right off this path down a double hedged bridleway. Cross an estate road and continue on to the road and the church.

❿ Cross over and turn right down an elevated walkway back to your car.

GREAT SALING

Length: 4½ miles

<table>
<tr><td>

Getting there: From the west join the A120; a few miles east of Great Dunmow turn left by the Saling Oak pub and Great Saling is 2 miles to the north. From the east, drive on the A120

</td><td>

west of Braintree, turning right at the Saling Oak pub.

Parking: Just beyond the White Hart pub there is an estate road on the right which will accom-

</td><td>

modate a car or two.

Map: OS Landranger – Chelmsford and Harlow 167 (GR 701254).

</td></tr>
</table>

Great Saling village lies tucked away in the midst of picturesque scenery. There is a Hall whose gardens to this day are of great interest, though not generally open to the public, and the church is a 14th century building much restored, with a traceried font and some roof beams of the 15th century. Shining in the tower window is a red robed St James, to whom the church is dedicated.

Saling Hall is a Grade II Listed Building of Special Architectural or Historical Interest, as are Mounts Farmhouse, Picots Farmhouse and its adjoining barn. The Hall is less elderly than the church though still 300 years old. It is a noble building

FOOD and DRINK

In the White Hart excellent food and drink is provided. In addition to the bar food there is a restaurant at the rear in what was once a bakehouse. Telephone: 01371 850341.

with two gabled wings. The White Hart is of architectural interest too, being of Tudor times with a timbered gallery in the saloon bar. On the green opposite are the remains of what was claimed to be the largest smooth leaved elm in the world. Alas, it was destroyed by Dutch elm disease in 1974.

For nearly a hundred years life in the villages hereabouts was transformed by the craft of straw plaiting. The craft was started about 1790. When established the industry proved a source of unheard of wealth to the poorer people. By 1800 a clever girl could earn as much as a guinea a week and the ladies of the parish began to complain that domestic labour was becoming impossible to obtain. Nearly all the women, girls and even some men were employed. They could be seen walking the lanes busily plaiting with a roll of finished plait under one arm and a bunch of split straw under the other. In the late 19th century the trade faded away, mainly due to cheap imports.

In 1943 a new airfield, RAF Great Saling, was opened as a US air base. Very soon the field was renamed Andrews Field in honour of General Andrews of the US Air Force. As a bombing unit it was very successful but in 1944 relocated in France for better access to German targets. The field was then occupied by British Fighter Command. After victory in Europe the airfield closed down in December 1945. In 1972 Clive Harvey, who farmed the field, got approval for light aircraft to use the field.

History, ancient and modern, is all around you on this attractive walk. Woods and field paths take you out past old fishponds and through a lovely uncultivated area to Yarney Wood. A delightful path descends by a stream, bringing you back into the village. You may recognise some scenes, as part of the *Lovejoy* television series was filmed locally.

THE WALK

❶ From the village green near the White Hart turn right off the main road, walking north-east and then round to the south-east.

❷ After 300 yards leave the road by a footpath sign and walk south along the edge of a field. When you reach a small wood on your left take the path inside the wood, bearing left to a gate at the far edge of the wood. Cross over the field making for another gate opposite. Through the gate continue in this direction to a larger crossing track.

❸ Turn left along this and continue along

PLACES of INTEREST

Not far from the village at 'The Waterings', Dunmow Road, Felsted (Telephone: 01371 820415) Arthur Clarke has a collection of **Fairgrounds and Dutch Street Organs**. Arthur will happily open up to show some of these but only by previous arrangement on the telephone.

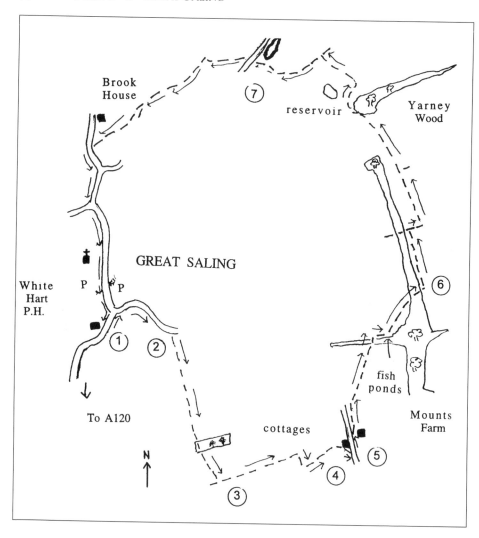

this track by a field and round to the right. Exit from the field and turn left in the next field with a hedge on your left.

❹ At the corner of this field turn right in front of two houses and soon left out to a road.

❺ Turn left past Mounts Farm. After a few yards, at a concrete public footpath sign, leave the road to the right, walking north-east to reach a track beside a small wood. Turn right following this track downhill. The track passes some old fishponds. At the field corner turn left for a few yards. Watch out for a narrow path leading north and crossing a bridge to the other side of the wood.

The village pub.

❻ A waymark points to the left. Follow this to join another footpath and turn right with it for a few yards. Soon turn left, walking north-west through a delightful uncultivated area to Yarney Wood on the right. Pass a reservoir on your left, turning right to cross a stile and follow the fence on your left to a gate by a farm road.

❼ Cross the road and enter the field opposite. Pass down a steepish descent to a pasture field. A lovely path this, between a stream on your right and a high plateau on your left. Approaching Brook House on your right, continue on your line in a countryside access area to a road at the rear of the gardens of some houses.

Turn left along the road up a slope and into Great Saling village.

WALK 9

LITTLE WALTHAM

Length: 3¾ miles

Getting there: From Chelmsford, Little Waltham is signposted from the A130 after Broomfield. From Great Dunmow the same road (A130) gets you there off the Chelmsford bypass and

from Braintree the A131 leads to the same point.

Parking: There is a village car park (free) between the church and the main street. It is sign-

posted next to the Memorial Hall.

Map: OS Landranger – Chelmsford and Harlow 167 (GR 711128).

Less than 4 miles from the centre of Chelmsford, Little Waltham is a lovely spot to visit and explore on foot, especially since bypassed by the A130. The walk passes a house in the village which was built in the 15th century, and many of the farms and cottages are from the 16th and 17th century. A visit to the church will

reveal a nave from Norman times and the spacious timber porch is of Tudor origin.

This relaxing walk crosses and recrosses the Chelmer along its length. Leaving the village behind, you take quiet paths across country to the delightfully named Larks Lane and Sparrowhawk Wood. The return is via Croxton Mill, on the riverside.

THE WALK

❶ Leave the village car park the way you entered and turn right along the road past a fine chestnut tree. Turn left down The Street passing the Post Office and Stores on your right. Pass the Congregational church and the quaintly named Romanys on your left. The road crosses the Chelmer.

❷ Turn right off the road opposite a house called The Times. The concrete public footpath sign is there but is partly hidden in ivy. Cross the pebble path into a field and carry straight on down a track. Follow the track to a gate leading alongside the river. Turn left under a bridge carrying the road above.

❸ Turn left and follow the road at your left side to a footpath sign.

❹ Here turn right down concrete steps into a field. Aim to the left of two willow trees and a pill box at a field corner opposite and cross an earth bridge. From here cross a second field to the Windmill restaurant ahead to the right of two poplar trees. When you reach the road observe the public footpath sign with a butterfly etched in yellow on it. This is the logo adopted by the Chelmsford Borough Council as part of their praiseworthy endeavours to make all

the rights of way in the Borough as good as they should be.

❺ Turn right past the Windmill.

❻ At a wide opening on your left follow the public footpath sign on the field edge pointing south-west. Pass behind a house and a garden, cross a bridge. Turn right at a footpath sign and follow the path with a hedge on your right.

❼ At the end of the field turn right along a farm track with a hedge and ditch on your left to a field corner.

❽ Here turn left over a bridge. Take the crossfield path south-east to the projecting corner of the facing hedge and continue straight on to a road (Larks Lane).

❾ Turn right along the lane, until the lane swings to the right.

❿ Turn left by a concrete footpath sign to reach Sparrowhawk Wood. Turn left alongside the wood and right at a footpath sign. At the end of the wood go straight on across the field to an oak by a bridge. Bear slightly to the left with a hedge and ditch on your right. Keep to the hedge when the track turns left. Cross a stile and go straight on to a road at a concrete footpath sign.

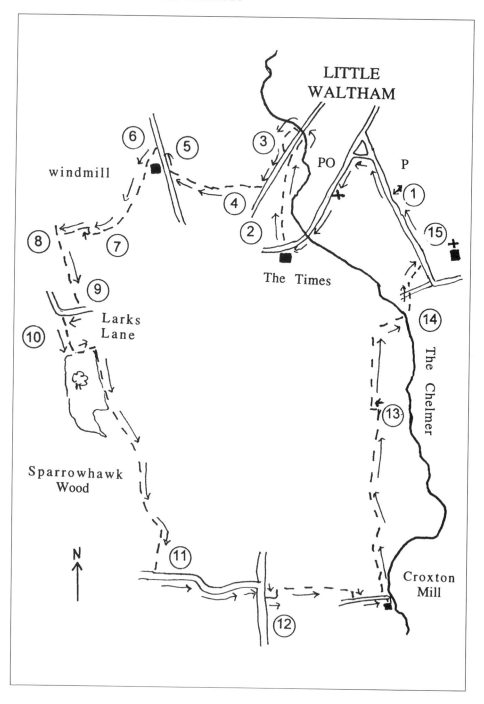

The Street, Little Waltham.

❶❶ Turn left along the road for 400 yards, to the A131. Cross with great care, and turn right for a few yards to a concrete footpath sign.

❶❷ Turn left down the side of gardens and a hedge. Finally the path loops to the right and then turns left onto a lane. Just before reaching Croxton Mill by the river Chelmer, turn left over a stile and cross a meadow to another stile and a well worn path.

❶❸ Cross the bridge on your left and walk right along the field edge. At the field

corner turn right with the public footpath sign. Do not turn left but continue to a large concrete bridge over the Chelmer.

❶❹ Immediately after crossing turn left and follow the path through the trees. Turn half right over a lawn to a gap and cross the stile. Cross the lane to another stile. Here take the path diagonally to your right across an open field and reach the road through a small clump of bushes and trees.

❶❺ Turn left along the road for 200 yards back to the car park.

FOBBING

Length: 3 miles

Getting there: From the A13/A176 junction, Five Bells Roundabout, just south of Basildon take the country road marked Fobbing 1 mile. As you approach the village you will see the tower of the church, head for this.

Parking: Is available outside St Michael's church on the road.

Map: OS Landranger – The Thames Estuary 178 (GR 718838).

This delightful village on a hill is a complex mixture of new and old. Saxon remains have been found in the church and its grey Norman tower is a landmark for miles. In 1381 Fobbing became famous for its part in the revolt against the new poll tax levy. Thomas Baker was among the rebels who led the first riots because they felt they had already paid their share of the tax and would pay no more. Essex men played a prominent part in the Peasants Revolt that followed, ending with the death of their Kentish leader Wat Tyler a few months later.

This delightful walk takes you toward Fobbing Marsh where you can see South

Benfleet and Southend in the distance. As you climb over the ridge you then get views of the Thames and the oil refineries on its banks. A high path takes you past large fishing ponds. Around the delightful Corringham Hall area time seems to have stood still, and you may like to time your walk so that you arrive in Corringham for a drink or a meal!

THE WALK

❶ Walk down the road to enter St Michael's churchyard by the side gate. Pass the beautiful carved porch and take a path half-right downhill to a metal gate. Turn left and continue on downhill on the road. Ignore the footpath sign to Iron Hatch. Take the footpath sign to Pitsea and go through the five-bar gate towards old farm buildings to a concrete area. The stile is at the end of the brick wall. Cross the paddock to a second stile. Here a handmade sign confirms your route.

❷ After about 10 yards turn left and walk uphill to join a track. Turn right on the track, walk under power lines and just before the track turns left, enter the field on your left and walk with a ditch on your right. As this ditch widens the path crosses the field left, going almost due north towards the houses and power line. This

path is normally reinstated by the local farmer. When you come to the stream turn right along the hedge and enter the meadow ahead. There is a pond area with lots of reeds to your right. Walk through this meadow and join a track at the field edge just to the left of the pond. The track turns left in this next field as you walk on to a junction of three paths marked by a high footpath sign.

❸ Take the track uphill to the houses and you will join the road where there is a footpath sign. You will find the track is named Marshes Lane. Turn left on the main road and enjoy the views back over the marshes.

❹ Turn right just after No 1 Fishers Cottages and walk on the path up beside their back garden. This takes you on a hedged path to a junction with another track. Turn left onto this new path and go through the wide gap in the hedge to enjoy super views over Corringham works. The well walked path continues downhill with a hedge on your left. At a footpath sign keep on path number 23 through the hedge and on down to a stile and busy road.

❺ Cross with care and join footpath 22 to Corringham. Walk up the concrete road. Just before a gate you will see a footpath

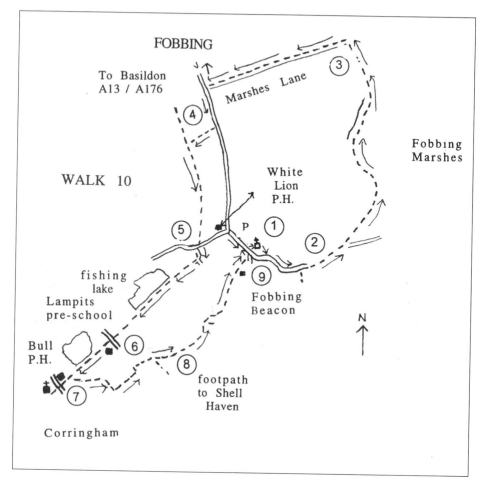

FOBBING

To Basildon
A13 / A176

Marshes Lane

WALK 10

White
Lion
P.H.

Fobbing
Marshes

fishing
lake
Lampits
pre-school

Fobbing
Beacon

N

Bull
P.H.

footpath
to Shell
Haven

Corringham

sign beside a wire fence. Turn right up this beside executive houses. Do not take the well marked cross-field path at this point. Go through the field edge and cross the stile ahead. The path continues with fences on both sides and you pass above a playing field on your left and a fishing lake on your right.

❻ Cross the road and take the path to the right of Lampits Pre School. Pass a further pond and paddock on your way under the

wooden beam and out on the road by the Bull pub and Corringham church and Hall Farm. A chance of a rest and refreshments if you have timed your walk right!

❼ When you have had a good look round, return to the footpath you came on and make your way back to the wooden beam. The footpath sign is marked '24 Fobbing' and points the way over a couple of stiles into a paddock. Cross the paddock to a stile on the far side. Turn right to walk between

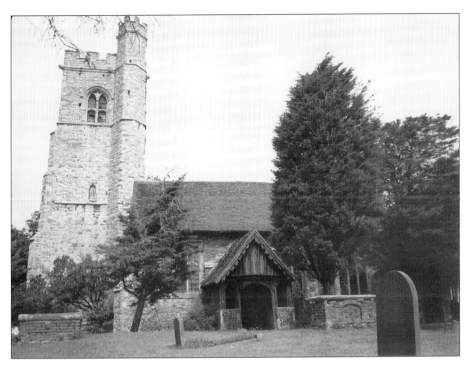

St Michael's church.

two fences, and again note the good views of the Thames. At the end of this path turn left onto a track that leads downhill with a fence on your left. Turn left and then right onto a gravel road by the school. Ignore the footpath sign to Shell Haven and keep right of the car park slightly downhill to a five-bar metal gate.

❽ Cross the fields ahead and follow the path with a pond on your left. At the end of the pond follow it round left to join another path at the mesh fence. Turn right and at footpath sign '13 Shell Haven' take the path north-east. Ignore a stile on your right and follow the path toward the church high above you. This slightly rough scrub path goes under some trees, then slightly left as you go uphill. You go over a crossing path, still uphill, toward Fobbing Beacon.

❾ Turn left and pass behind the beacon (north-west) and head downhill to a house roof in the distance. At a fence turn right and walk under the power line. The path now goes uphill to a kissing gate to the right of a metal gate and you come out by the footpath sign in Wharf Road. Walk out onto the road ahead and your car is just to the left by the church.

EAST HANNINGFIELD

Length: 5 ½ miles

Getting there: East Hanningfield lies south-east of Chelmsford. From the north or west take the A12 to its junction with the A130. Take the A130 south to Howe Green and then turn left on to East Hanningfield Road till you come to the village. From the south take the A130 north till 1 mile past Rettendon, turn right into Pan Lane; this leads to the village centre.

Parking: In the village hall car park which is signposted opposite the church, on your right if coming south or left and left again from Pan Lane.

Map: OS Landranger – Chelmsford and Harlow 167 (GR 770012).

East Hanningfield is a typical country village. A neat wide green runs alongside the main street. On this are two public houses, a church and a police station. The post office is in the car park and the school and village hall are right at the centre of the village, all essential to thriving village life.

I am told the vicar's garden has the oldest well in the country, which is 480 feet deep. There are even the ruins of a medieval church a mile outside the village.

There is a story that a 600 year old wall painting of great value showing Adam with his spade, Eve with her spindle and Catherine with her wheel, laid for many years in the ruin exposed to the open sky till given a new home in the Victoria and Albert Museum.

This lovely three village walk goes by the St Peter's Way to the outskirts of Bicknacre, through the woods to Woodham Ferrers and then over the magnificent hills back to East Hanningfield.

THE WALK

❶ From the car park return to the road, cross with care and turn right on a tarred path. About half-way along the green turn left at the footpath sign and walk through Cobb's. Pass a 10mph sign with a yellow arrow and the sign 'No public bridleway'. There is an arrow on the power line pole. Ignore the stile on the left and walk between the bungalows and the production sheds. An arrow directs you over a stile and then on to a concrete road. Walk left of a wire link fence on a tarred road.

❷ At the junction go straight on, following the arrows into a fenced track. You pass the last hen houses. Walk with the hedge on your right. Half-way along this field at the footpath sign the path goes slightly left into the field to a stile (if this is overgrown the locals tend to walk up the hedge line, turning left at a line of oaks). The stile is just past the pond.

❸ Walk between the fence and hedge till you cross a bridge to enter Leighams Farm. The path goes left, then right, then left at the end of the paddock. Continue round buildings, passing the horses' exercise machine, and cross the stile and bridge ahead. Walk with a field hedge on your left and just before the road, turn left down a long green bridleway.

❹ Just before the houses, turn right to enter the village playing field. Walk straight across to the gate marked 'Dog Exercise Area'. Through the gate follow the locals' route by keeping the hedge on your right till you come to the gate and the road.

❺ Turn left and walk till nearly opposite the Brewers Arms. Cross the road with care and go down the bridleway. A path joins from the left, then a footpath sign shows the right turn. It has a St Peter's Way sign plus a blue arrow. At Thrift Wood continue ahead on a wide gravel track, blue arrows show the way. At the end of the wood

Woodham Ferrers.

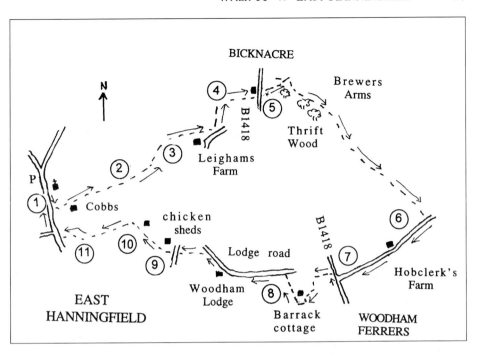

continue straight ahead with a ditch on your right. The mile long path goes straight ahead through three gates, then turns slightly right to the road.

❻ At the footpath sign on the road turn right. Walk past Hobclerk's Farm as you come to the B1418. Turn right and then just past the phone box, left at the footpath sign.

❼ The track goes to Barrack Cottage. Just before the cottage turn left up a grass track that takes you round the back garden. Continue right round to the west of the house and walk back past it on a 300 yard track to the road.

❽ Turn left along Lodge Road passing Woodham Lodge about one third of the

way along. Take a left turn at the footpath sign, on this westerly path to the road.

❾ Cross over the road to a bridleway sign and walk up the track to a wooden footpath sign by the gate. Bear left at the chicken sheds onto a gravel track.

❿ As the track turns right, take the wide cross-field path left as indicated on the direction post. Between two oak trees at the next direction post, cross the bridge and continue towards houses over the next field.

⓫ A bridge and wobbly stile take you into your last field. Walk half-right on a well marked path to a stile and fence that brings you out onto the road opposite the Windmill pub. Turn right and make your way back to your car.

GOSFIELD

Length: 3¼ miles

Gosfield is a beautiful village. The scene is set by Gosfield Hall which stands in grounds rich in cedars and shrubberies. Enclosed in the parklands is a magnificent lake of 50 acres now given over to water sports and swimming. Queen Elizabeth I did indeed sleep here in the Hall as the guest of Lord Rich, who at the time owned a great part of the county.

Gosfield church stands in a corner of

moniously, some backing onto the grounds of the great house. By the main road is a small green area with bench seats to rest awhile. Nearby is a post office and stores which may supply your immediate needs.

This easy walk takes you over rolling countryside to Highwoods Farm, then back through a nature reserve to the village and on to Gosfield Hall before crossing the fields back to the church.

the park. Its foundations are much older than the Hall. The present building dates from 1435. The monumental brass of Sir Thomas Rolfe is one of the best in the county.

The cottages in the village blend har-

THE WALK

❶ From the church turn right along the pavement. At a concrete public footpath signpost numbered 15, enter the field on the left and walk beside the hedge on your right.

Gosfield Hall.

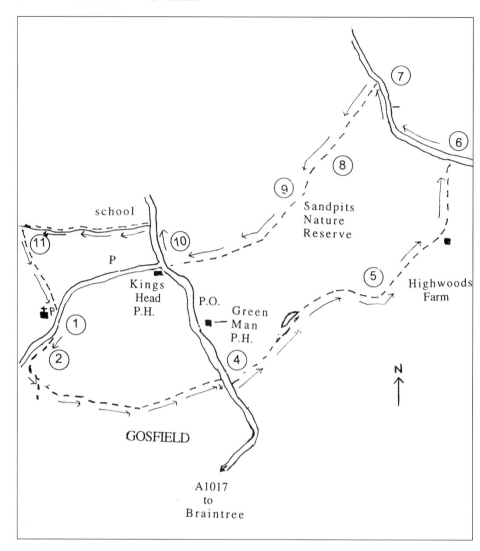

❷ At the field corner, with a glimpse of the lake on your right, turn left and follow the edge to a tall TV aerial.

❸ Turn left across the field aiming to the right of a solitary oak tree. At the end of the field cross a stile and continue up a track. Near a gate veer to the left by a

waymark and cross another stile.

❹ Cross the road with care, and turn right downhill for a few yards. Just past a cottage garden turn left up a broad track with house gardens on either side. As you enter a field turn left along the edge and then right at the corner. Ignore a bridge on the

PLACES of INTEREST

Four miles north of Gosfield by the A1017 and the A604 is the **Colne Valley Steam Railway** at Castle Hedingham, which enthusiasts of all ages may wish to visit. It is ideal for a weekend family outing and the museum can be visited daily. Rides on the carriages hauled by one of many steam locos are possible on Sunday from 12 noon to 4 pm. During the summer school holidays only, rides are also available on Tuesday, Wednesday and Thursday, again from 12 noon till 4 pm. Telephone: 01787 461174.

left leading into the woods to walk between two fields. The path continues with trees on the left past a pond and reaches a broad track.

❺ Here turn left towards Highwoods Farm. Bear left up a track to a public footpath sign at a road.

❻ Turn left for 500 yards.

❼ Coming to a wood ahead, turn left by a concrete public footpath sign and follow first the wood then a ditch on your right. The path continues straight on across two large fields.

❽ Cross a stile into woods to a waymark at a clearing.

❾ Enter a fence gap to the Sandpits nature reserve. Turn right at the waymark to the village.

❿ At the road opposite the King's Head turn right along the main road, crossing left into Hall Lane marked to the golf club and police station.

⓫ Just before white fencing at Gosfield Hall turn left, aiming to the left of the church. In 100 yards you are back at your car.

BATTLESBRIDGE

Length: 3¾ miles

Getting there: Take the A130 north from the A127 between Basildon and Southend and just past Rawreth follow the signs right to Battlesbridge. From Chelmsford on the A12 take the A130 south till you have just passed Rettendon Turnpike (junction of A130 and A132). Battlesbridge is again well signed left with large brown 'Battlesbridge Antiques Centre' signs.

Parking: There is ample parking outside the antiques centre but they do ask for you to avoid parking by the delivery doors as these are in frequent use.

Map: OS Landranger – Chelmsford and Harlow 167 (GR 781947).

Battlesbridge is an exciting mixture of new and old situated almost at the end of the navigable part of the river Crouch. It is still visited by quite large vessels which moor outside the old mill, which is now part of the large antiques and craft industry.

There is both glamour and purpose to a visit here – be it an article for the home or an interesting present for a friend you are sure to find something here that fits the bill.

The old village has a range of interesting houses and you pass these on the walk out, where views downstream on the river Crouch stretch as far as the new town of South Woodham Ferrers. You can enjoy the rural nature of the area, with horses below you in fields on your side of the river and an open air pig farm on the south bank, on your way to Marks Farm. On a clear day spectacular views over Woodham Ferrers, Hyde Hall, Rettendon, Rettendon Place and Wickford await you before you return to the bustle of Battlesbridge.

THE WALK

❶ From the car park take the bridge just to the left of the Barge Inn and cross into the rear car park of Cromwell antiques shop and cafe. Head up the right-hand side and out onto Maltings Road.

❷ Turn right and walk down this tarmac road till just before Gosse's Farm. On the lane junction you will see on the right three steps at a footpath sign. Go up these and on to the river wall. Walk round the edge of Harveys factory, passing under a low bar. You get good views of the river and back to the mill.

❸ The path on the river wall eventually goes slightly inland. Ignore a five-bar gate and climb up into a field. Turn right and head along the edge of the field to a short direction post at the right-hand corner of this field. At the post turn left towards the power lines going up the field edge on a somewhat rough and concrete lump-strewn path. You will be pleased when half-way along the field you find yourself on a fine firm farm track. Time to look over towards Bushey Hill and the new town on your right.

❹ Follow the track up and over the railway line and cross the sometimes busy new road that may not be shown on your map. Cross over the stile at the footpath sign with the yellow butterfly, a reminder you are in the Chelmsford district. The track continues ahead and you will pass on your left a super brick wall that seems to have no purpose, on your way to the old B1012.

❺ Turn right and walk on the path beside the road for 400 yards until you reach W. D. Smith & Son Nurseries. Cross the road with care and turn left up Rectory Lane. As you climb you pass the amusingly named 'Stony Broke'. Ignore the crossing path and climb to the top of the road. You will be rewarded with super views. The track continues past Frelins Farm to Marks Farm. A direction post confirms your route

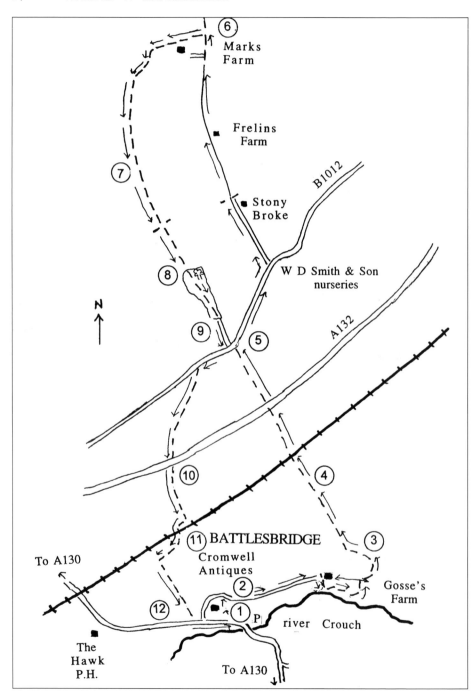

Friendly residents.

is straight ahead, walking north just east of the farm drive.

❻ At a five-bar gate and footpath sign, turn left and climb over a three-rung metal stile. Walk up the field edge with a wire fence on your left. At the next four-bar stile, cross then turn left and immediately cross a second four-bar metal stile (no yellow arrow points this way but it is your path). Walk uphill beside a wire fence. You pass to the west of Marks Farm and continue to a field corner where a yellow arrow on a short post indicates you turn right. Half-way along this next field edge turn left and cross the stile. The track going straight across the next field is normally well marked by previous walkers.

Ahead you cross another stile into a field with a lot of thistles. This field goes to a point and at the point you turn right to cross a stile and bridge into a large field.

❼ Turn left and climb uphill with a hedge on your left. At the crest of the hill cross a crossing path and walk on just to the right of a row of oak trees, downhill towards the wood.

❽ Enter the centre of the wood and walk downhill on a well marked track, later passing a wire fence on your left. Now head for the wooden fence ahead. At the fence turn left and cross a bridge into a fenced path between gardens that leads to a stile and road.

❾ Walk ahead down this road to the B1012. Turn right and cross with care. Opposite the repair garage there is a footpath sign on your left. Cross the stile into a field that appears to be set aside. Your route half-left to the field corner in the centre of the field is rough, so walk along the right-hand field edge as the locals do till a mown track takes you left to a bridge and stile at the field corner. Cross into the next field and you will see the cars on the road ahead. There is no direct route to the next stile so I suggest you walk slightly right through the blue five-bar gate in the fence, not shown on your map, then half-left back to the stile.

❿ Cross the busy A132 to a concrete footpath sign and stile. The path goes cross-field to the next field edge by a pylon, then turns left to the far hedge and a short marker post. At the corner turn right and follow with the hedge on the left till you reach a very high white marker post and stile. Turn left over the stile and cross the railway bridge.

⓫ Turn right into the sports field and walk with a hedge on the right till you go through the next hedge. Turn left down the field edge to a very high stile. A path leads between fenced gardens to the front of the properties and through a kissing gate to Cromwell antiques.

⓬ Walk out towards the main road, turn left and pass Battlesbridge Free church on your return to the car park.

GREAT BRAXTED

Length: 5 miles

Getting there: From the A12 at Rivenhall End (between Witham and Colchester) take the signs for Great Braxted. About 2 miles along country roads brings you	to the village centre. Parking: On a quiet road outside the post office or at the bottle bank (see 3 on the walk).	Map: OS Landranger – Colchester and the Blackwater 168 (GR 862142).

Great Braxted is a very small, quiet village tucked between Witham and Tiptree, on land occupied by ancient Britons before the Romans came. Unusually, the main long street of the village centre is separated by over a mile from Great Braxted Hall and the Norman church. Here lie the remains of the 7th

century Saxon King Sebert and this is also the church where Christopher Martin, treasurer on the *Mayflower*, married in 1607. Braxted Park, on the other hand, is famous for its brick wall, the longest I have ever seen.

The village is situated on the top of a ridge and the superb views as you walk

FOOD and DRINK

There is only one pub in the village but a warm welcome awaits you at the Du Cane Arms. A range of beers and ciders are on hand pump, and a wide range of freshly cooked pub food is available. If you want a real treat see if the fish in beer batter is on the menu. You may even want to book a later meal in their excellent restaurant. Telephone: 01621 891697.

stretch over several valleys, down over the Blackwater to Witham. Again, as the river swings round, you can see from Langford to Maldon from Beacon Hill. I have sat here and watched the famous sailing barges making their way along the river a good 3 miles away. As you descend past Scripps Farm you walk into Spickets Brook valley, then over to Penny's Brook valley. The stream accompanies you as you turn back towards Great Braxted, making this a very pleasurable ramble.

THE WALK

❶ Take the path between the pub and R & J Coachworks to walk beside a house. Ignore the path going sharp right and follow the garden fence onto a path that swings first left, then right through about ⅓ mile of wilderness woodland. Take the main track at all times and you will find yourself wandering within a few feet of the fences to your right, then left. As you drop further down it becomes more wooded and someone has tied a blue rope high in an oak tree right over the path. Head for the bottom right-hand side of this wood and the path then suddenly turns a final sharp left to the road and a direction post well covered in greenery.

❷ Turn left and walk this quiet road up past Sexton's Farm to the bottle bank.

❸ At the bottle bank junction turn right onto a road with views down from the ridge on both sides. Continue to walk past Strowling Wood, which unfortunately is private, to a stile and gate by the footpath sign.

❹ Cross into the field and walk ahead with the wood on your left. To your far right in some trees is the beautifully named Cock-a-Bevis cottage. As you descend you come to a soft fruit farm, a stile, three steps and a bridge that leads you out onto busy Mountains Road.

❺ Do take care as you turn right and walk to Beacon Hill. There is a seat near the road junction so why not take a short break here and admire the view. Now take the left turn into Goat Lodge Road. The wide grass verge on the right gets you off the road.

❻ After 300 yards, at the footpath sign turn left down a gravel track. You will pass just to the right of Scripps Farm which in 1997 was greatly enlarged. The track continues to the busy Maldon Road.

❼ Cross with care to Beckingham Road almost opposite and walk through Spickets Brook valley, passing Foresters Park Golf Club, Paynes Farm built in 1777 and Stans Coaches, to Totham Hill Green. Turn left onto the green and you will find another bench for a well earned rest, then walk on for 300 yards.

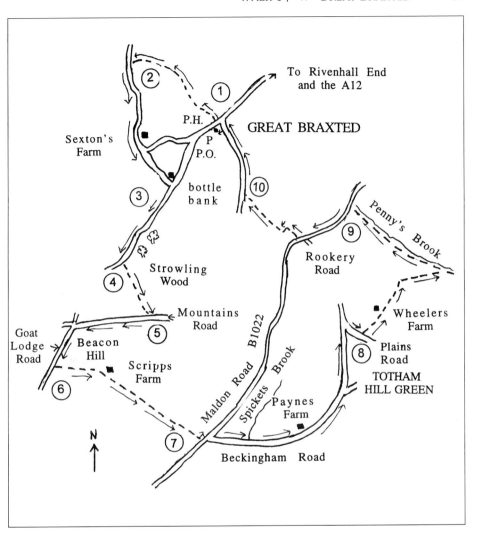

8 At a junction turn right into Plains Road. Then 100 yards on, turn left at a footpath sign up the drive of Wheelers Farm. Where the gravel drive goes into the farm you continue straight ahead between two hedges till you come to an open field. Turn left with a hedge on your left to pass under six oak trees as the path swings round to the right. Continue ahead till you come to a concrete bridge. Turn left before the bridge and walk up the left-hand side of Penny's Brook. At the field corner bear right to enter a hedged track to finish uphill beside Maldon Road.

9 Turn left and walk up the grass verge till it runs out, then cross with care onto the verge on the right. Continue in the same

The village pub.

direction. There is a very narrow bit opposite Rookery Road but the stile is just 4 yards further on your right. Cross into a field with a fence on your left. Follow this round the corner and then 10 yards further on, turn right to cross a large field. The track here is usually well defined and you head for the facing hedge corner. On reaching the hedge continue with this on your right. At the end of the hedge turn left to the footpath sign and the road.

PLACES of INTEREST

Maldon is a lovely town to explore, every street seeming to lead you down to the fascinating quayside. A walk in Promenade Park gives you exceptional views of the river. Telephone: Maldon Tourist Information Centre on 01621 856503.

🔟 Turn right and walk uphill. You will soon see the village of Great Braxted set out in front of you. At the T-junction turn left to find your car.

WORMINGFORD

Length: 4¼ miles

Getting there: From the A604 in Fordstreet (between Colchester and Halstead) take the road north through Fordham to the B1508. Turn right for about ½ mile, and at the Old Queen's	Head turn left up the concrete drive to the village hall car park. Parking: Available at the village hall. Also at a small park at the	end of Downs Road off Church Road. Map: OS Landranger – Colchester and the Blackwater 168 (GR 934316).

Wormingford is a village in two parts. This fascinating walk starts through the village playing field with its children's climbing frames, then makes its way through a residential area where there is a mixture of properties of all ages, with the post office nearby. Walking right past the glider club, there is plenty going on to watch.

The thrilling panorama over the Stour valley then comes into view. In 1836 down by the river Stour a large mound containing many hundreds of urns in parallel rows was discovered. It is thought to be a Bronze Age cemetery, but at the time all the pots were smashed and covered with earth in the field.

You then pass the weir famous as being the home of the Wormingford dragon. Legend tells us this beast ate maidens who tried to pass that way!

Walking uphill to the 13th century church, this is very much the smaller part of the village but to my mind one of the prettiest places to look round. The well spaced houses are very old and each one has many interesting features. Even the textures of the walls are a work of art. In the church find the stained glass window that shows the dragon crocodile. In the graveyard, by a holly tree in the far hedge lies John Nash the painter, who lived in the village for many years and died here in 1977. John Constable's uncles are said to be buried nearby.

Passing the unique flintstone village school, more superb views of the Stour valley follow as you walk round The Grange on your way back to the car.

THE WALK

❶ Take the path between the houses and the village hall. Note the old beacon. Continue down the path facing you and turn left at the next road, crossing to the path on the right-hand side past Newhouse Farm to a busy road.

❷ Cross the B1508 to a footpath sign and a metal gate with built-in stile. The path follows to the left of a ditch. Cross an earth bridge and go right and left round the field edge to the footpath sign at the road.

❸ Turn left and make for the footpath sign. Watch out for fast cars here. Just before the sign turn right and follow the locals' route up a concrete drive. It bends left to pass in front of the clubhouse for the gliding club.

❹ Turn right at the joining track. You should spot the yellow waymark here. Go about half-way up the track, then take a path right between the last two trees of a line that continues right out into the field. Walk this then go left round the corner. Continue on this path till you come to a concrete track coming in at a 45° angle from your right.

❺ Walk up this track and enjoy the super views. At the farm buildings turn left to walk to a hedge and direction post. Take the track on your right to pass the triangulation point used by the Ordnance Survey in map making.

❻ Turn left on the busy B1508 to go under cables and slightly downhill till you come to the second footpath sign high up on your right. Climb your way up to cross the stile.

❼ Turn left down the field edge to a yellow waymarked stile which you cross. Walk right beside the hedge towards a white gate

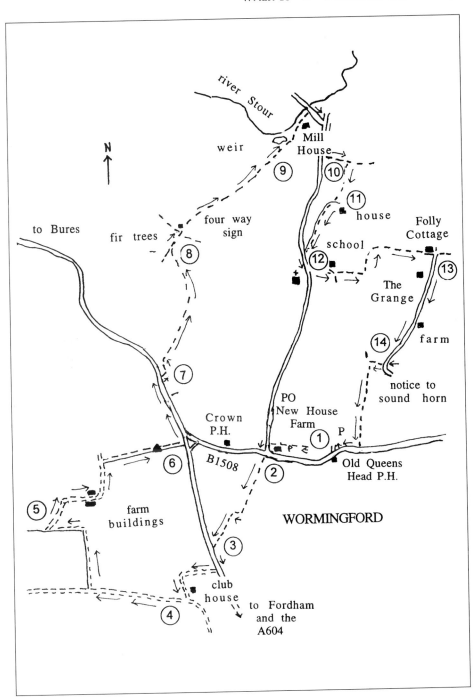

Mill House.

with a sign 'No Footpath'. Continue round the field edge to the second white gate. Turn left towards the fir trees. There are some cut logs here to sit on if you want a break.

8 Walk towards the fourway sign by the stile. Do not cross, but turn right towards the field corner. If the gate is closed climb the brown climbing rails and continue down the track ahead.

9 As a hedge joins from the right look for a stile on the left. Cross this and go right and left over an earth bridge. A home-made footpath sign on a tree lets you know you have found the right path. Head slightly right to a stile about half-way down a garden edge. Cross the stile into the garden of Mill House. Join the gravel track by the famous weir pond and walk out to the road. Turn right uphill on the road and bear right again at the bend.

10 Just as your legs begin to notice the climb you will see a footpath sign by a yellow salt box. Turn left along the gravel road to pass an interesting cottage. The dogs are secure in the back garden. At the end of the front garden take the waymark right, up a fenced path, and continue ahead through a small wood to an old brick shed.

11 Turn to the right before the private house and walk up their drive to come out on the road near the church. Turn left to go

PLACES of INTEREST

A few miles south-west is the impressive **Chappel Viaduct** and the **East Anglian Railway Museum** at Wakes Colne. There are regular Steam Days and many exhibits and displays. Open daily (telephone: 01206 242524).

and investigate the church. It's normally open. Retrace your steps to the footpath sign that also indicates the road to the school.

🄬 Take this road, enjoying the old buildings nearby as you go. The path is just to the right of the school. Go over a stile into a wide field. Your path is straight across to the yellow waymark, then left along the far hedge. Turn right and cross over two stiles to Folly Cottage and a junction of four paths.

🄭 Turn right at the waymark. Follow the farm road to pass The Grange on your right, and up the hill to pass a farm on your left. As you go downhill look for the sharp uphill left turn. Just at this point is a black farm gate. Ignore this and go right uphill on a narrow grass, hedged track to a stile.

🄮 Turn left onto the crossing path, to a corner of the field with a stile and waymark. Cross to the field edge and enter the next field that leads out to the road. Turn right, go past a few houses and rejoin the track back to the cars.

GREAT WAKERING

Length: 5 miles

Getting there: Great Wakering is right in the south-east corner of Essex, just to the north of Shoeburyness which is the most easterly part of Southend on Sea. You must approach by either of the two trunk roads, the A127 or the A130. On either of these follow the signs to Shoeburyness and then turn left where indicated to Great Wakering on the B1017. Drive along the High Street passing all four of the village's pubs, and turn left into Common Road.

Parking: Parking is suggested on the Common Road opposite the church.

Map: OS Landranger – The Thames Estuary 178 (GR 949876).

Great Wakering is famous for two things. Firstly, it is the gateway to Foulness Island which, though it has a church and the village of Churchend on it, is nevertheless a no-go military establishment. The second notable feature of Great Wakering is that nearby is a weather station. Records show that this is the driest station (least rainfall) in England and thus it is commonly said that Great Wakering is the driest place in the country!

The village has two churches in the

High Street. One is the church of the Peculiar People, an evangelical sect founded in the 19th century with a belief in the power of divine healing. The other is the parish church which is remarkable for its age and for a two-storey building which in the 15th century was attached to the Norman tower. It was added to shelter the priest who came to minister here from Beeleigh Priory.

There is plenty of interest, on land and water, on this walk. Cross Wakering Common towards the sea wall, then walk along the wall and by the creek round Mill Head to Fleet Head. Potton Island, another military establishment, is just across the water. It is then easy walking back to Great Wakering village.

THE WALK

❶ From the church walk on Common Road, passing a large pond on the left. Walk past some of a group of new houses on your right. Turn right off the road at a concrete public footpath sign, following a track across Wakering Common. Take notice of the power lines and generally follow these, walking east.

❷ Pass a pumping station on your left. After about ½ mile you come to a metal gate at the end of the Common track. There is a misleading sign here, 'Private Road No Bridleway'.

❸ Observe the Public Footpath sign. Yes, it is a public footpath to Oxenham Farm and yes, this is your route.

❹ When you reach the farm turn right at the end of the track. Pass along between houses on your left and barns on your right to climb up the steps to the sea wall.

❺ Turn left and walk along the wall (on your right is Rushley Island). Pass over four stiles as you go round Mill Head to leave the sea wall and follow the path fairly close to the creek. Rejoin the wall through Pottons Boat Yard. Pass the bridge to Potton Island. Continue for 150 years to a metal stile. Cross over and turn left to a metal gate at the bottom of the wall.

❻ Go through the gate to a well marked track and turn left along this, back across Fleet Head to the wall at Fleet Head Creek. About 200 yards onwards take the track left by a gate to Halfway House Farm. Do not follow the track round right to the farm

The pond at the start of the walk.

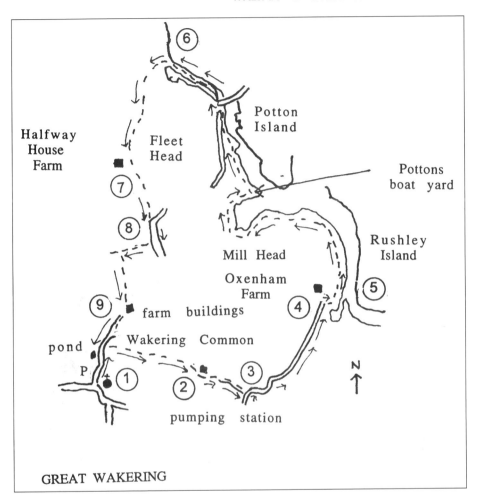

GREAT WAKERING

but turn left off it to a metal gate.

7 Go through this gate and follow the track round to the right. Cross a stile past two large ponds on to the road.

8 You soon come to a concrete public footpath sign. Turn right with this and when you come to a field boundary on your left, turn left along the far side of this.

9 Pass some farm buildings on your left hand and you soon come out to the Common Road by the entrance to Wakering Common. From here retrace your steps to your car.

LAYER DE LA HAYE

Length: 4¼ miles

Getting there: Layer de la Haye is south of Colchester. From there take the B1026 and after 2 miles turn left to Maypole Green, then right to head south to Friday Woods Car Park which is ¾ mile south on your left. Coming from the south take the

B1026 to Layer de la Haye village centre. Turn right at the Fox and then second left (Boundstead Road). Cross Roman river and the car park is on the right ¼ mile north of the river.

Parking: At Friday Woods Car Park.

Map: OS Landranger – Colchester and the Blackwater 168 (GR 986209).

Layer de la Haye is a small, quiet and somewhat spread out village with a mixture of properties, a large water works and the Fox Tavern at the crossroads as its centre. Layer de la Haye got part of its name from the little brook called Layer, but added the

name of a bygone worthy, one Maurice de Haia. Just to its south is Abberton Reservoir. The walk gives breathtaking views of this – it has its own nature reserve that is well worth a visit.

To the north is the garrison town of

Colchester which is said to be the oldest town in Essex. The beautiful Friday Wood is sometimes used for army training exercises. I remember watching with interest as soldiers radioed commands and manned patrols on an earlier visit here.

The walk takes you through the woods to cross the Roman river on a stout wooden bridge. Abberton church can be spotted as you walk below the reservoir wall. Then a short walk past a mixture of fine homes leads you down towards Mill House Farm, and delightful Mushroom Cottage and the weir.

Now follows a short uphill climb to bring you to horse riding country, and a delightful cross-field path back to Friday Wood. This walk has something for everyone – lovely woodland, a peaceful river and fine views.

THE WALK

❶ From your car follow the line south-east from the right-hand corner of the car park right out onto a heath area. Ignore two paths on your right and take the path that continues on the line you followed from the car park. After a few yards a path goes off left and another rutted path joins, ignore these. In a further few yards you will see a direction post on your right indicating a route off to your left. Take this, along the wide footpath. It goes slightly downhill. You will then see a path to your left – take this then look for the direction post showing you continue ahead up this slope to a crossing path.

❷ At the path and waymark turn right to go downhill on a concrete track under some tall Scots pine trees. Follow this track down over the stream and up the other side. As it bears left, ignore two paths on your right to follow the path ahead. It has become a wide gravel track. Ignore crossing paths and direction posts as you continue under the power lines to the white gate by the road.

❸ At the road continue ahead through a further gate to join a wide grass track. As you approach the fallen tree bear slightly right to pick up the parallel path about 10 feet to your right. This goes down into the woods to a small stile.

❹ Over the stile turn right up a gravel track (Cherry Tree Lane). After nearly a mile ignore the right turn to Park Farm, then as the track swings left go straight ahead downhill with the wood edge on your right. A track joins from your right

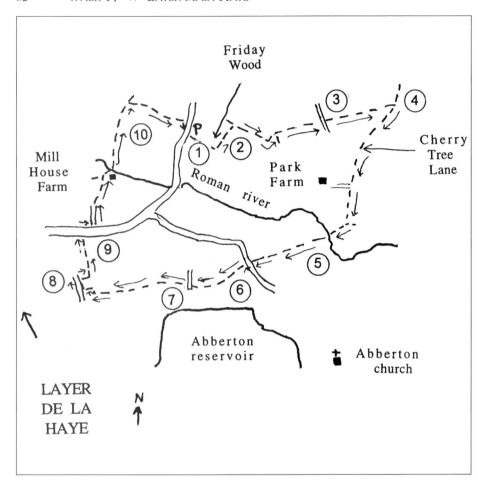

and you go slightly left on this down to a wooden bridge over Roman river. A nice spot to stop for a rest!

❺ Over the bridge go rightish with a sparse hedge on your right and dike on your left. As you reach the road go round the gate you face and through the wooden gate beside it. It has a sign, Roman river, hanging under the arm of the footpath sign. Cross the road with care to a stile made high by five runs of tight wire. It's just

next to a gate with a notice, Private Keep Out.

❻ Cross into the field and pass a wild bird sanctuary notice as you head half-right to a post with a footpath sign on it. This indicates a gap in the fence and you walk with a fence on your left to cross a stile. The next path takes you between the fence and hedge to the end of a concrete road.

❼ A right and left through at the end of

the road enables you to continue following the footpath sign. You enter a large field to walk near the ditch on the locals' path, on a long slow uphill climb. When you reach the field end turn right for 100 yards, then left for 100 yards to reach a road and footpath sign.

❽ Turn right and go uphill for 100 yards to a footpath sign. Turn right to enter the field you have recently left and go ahead for 100 yards between fence and hedge. As the hedge line goes left so do you for another slight climb. About half-way up turn and look over your right shoulder – what a view!

❾ Continue on this path till you reach the road. Turn right and when convenient cross to the other side. Your left turn is up Mill Road, first on a metalled road, later as you descend it becomes a gravel track. Go straight through the farm, passing Mushroom Cottage and the weir to cross a stile ahead.

❿ The gravel track turns left but you continue uphill on a grass track to cross a stile into a large horse jumping area. The hedge is on your left. At a fourway footpath sign turn right and follow the track ahead. Then at the fork take the right-hand track. This brings you to the road, to cross one final stile before you cross the road to your awaiting car.

BRADWELL ON SEA

Length: 6¼ miles

Getting there: Follow the brown signs to 'Bradwell Visitor Centre' as far as Latchingdon on the B1010. At the roundabout at the far end of the village take the road through the villages of Mayland and Steeple till after about 10 miles you get to a garage. Turn right, signed to Bradwell Village, drive into the village centre.

Parking: You can park on the road next to St Thomas's church, and outside school hours parking is possible on an area outside the village school. There is also a customer car park at the King's Head pub.

Map: OS Landranger – Colchester and the Blackwater 168 (GR 004068).

Once the site of the Roman fort of Othona, this beautiful village is packed with things to see. The parish church of St Thomas stands in the centre of the village. It has a solid brick tower and the most interesting walls, a mixture of flint and sandstone. At the southern entrance to the church is an ancient mounting block of five much-used stone steps, placed here for the convenience of parishioners who made the journey on horseback. At the end of the church wall stands the village lock-up.

FOOD and DRINK

There are two pubs and the Bradwell King's Head is just across the road from the parking place. Reasonably priced, home-cooked food is available in the old beamed bar or you may choose to eat in the bright new conservatory at the rear. A range of sandwiches, burgers, ploughman's, fish, ham, and steak dishes are available plus puddings like blackberry and apple pancake roll. Telephone: 01621 776224.

The grill and whipping posts can be seen by the door to this seven foot square building. I am told up to six offenders could be caged inside while as many as ten were tethered to posts outside.

The walk begins by taking you on a pilgrimage to St Peter's Ad Murum, the chapel founded by St Cedd in AD 654. It was built on the wall of the old Roman fort and has itself faced many changes of use. Till his death of the plague in 664 it was St Cedd's cathedral and it continued to be used for worship till the parish church of St Thomas was built in the 14th century. In Elizabethan times it was a simple navigation beacon and after years of neglect it became a barn. In 1920 it was restored and later renovated to its present simple splendour. Pilgrims from all over Essex come here on the first Saturday in July to celebrate the life of St Cedd, some of them walking the St Peter's Way from Ongar. We, ourselves, happened to visit once on this particular Saturday and have never shaken hands with so many ministers. They thought we were pilgrims when, in fact, we were just trying to have a quiet picnic!

The return route to Bradwell, along the sea wall goes past the power station nestling on the banks of the Blackwater. So keen are its workers to be environmentally accepted they have designed a nature trail and our walk treads this same trail for a short distance. There are reminders of the war years here too, both in the pillboxes along the way and the airfield you walk round. You pass the poignant RAF memorial as you return to the village.

THE WALK

❶ From the south entrance to St Thomas's church walk towards the lock-up. Note the picture map of the village just inside the church wall. Like the pilgrims of old, you walk through and out of the village. Passing a cemetery, then the Cricketers pub, go down this Roman road under phone cables and continue, passing a footpath sign on your way.

❷ A second footpath sign guides you into the car park for the chapel, at Eastlands Farm. Go though the kissing gate and up the stony path to the chapel. Just a few yards away to the right and hidden by the trees is Linnett's Cottage. It was the home of Walter Linnett, a wildfowler and fisherman. He lived in this solitary cottage till his death in 1958. If you make a detour down there, tread quietly as it's now Bradwell Bird Observatory.

PLACES of INTEREST

Bradwell Power Station has a hi-tech visitor centre, exhibition hall and guided tours. Admission free. Telephone: 01621 873395.

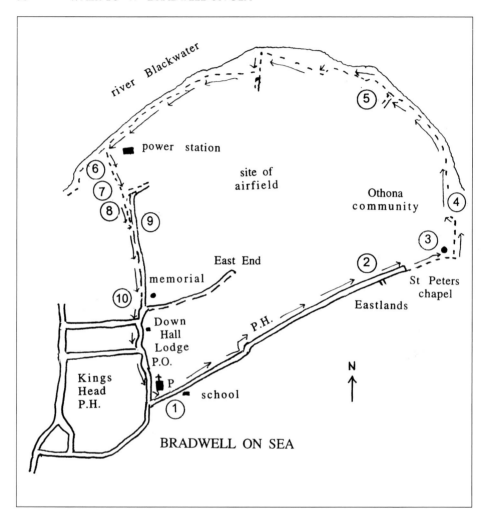

BRADWELL ON SEA

❸ Walk past St Peter's chapel, downhill slightly, toward Cockle Spit Nature Reserve. Turn left, following the well trodden path till you reach and climb a small set of stairs. To your left is Othona Community, founded in 1946 to follow a lifestyle of work, worship, study and play.

❹ At the footpath sign take the high gravel path that leads to the beach and sea wall. If the tide is right it is possible to bathe from here but please follow any warning signs placed along your deviation from the route.

❺ Where the concreted sea wall runs out just take a couple of steps to your left and immediately rejoin the grass-covered continuation of the route. To your left you will be able to pick out buildings that were

St Peter's chapel.

once part of Bradwell Bay airfield, operational from November 1941 to 1945. There are several tracks leading towards this area but all are private. The footpath follows the sea wall. The views over the Blackwater are of Brightlingsea, Mersea Island and Tollesbury, working from right to left. You then pass a magnox display board.

❻ Just after the waterbreak in the Blackwater channel ends you will see a path sloping down to cross an earth bridge. A power station arrow indicates the route. A path with a fence on the right-hand side leads to a green gate at the field edge. Go past this gate onto the gravel road.

❼ Walk up the road passing boarded cottages, one named Lodestone. You now come to an open area. Ahead are some bushes.

❽ At the bushes look for a post with a yellow footpath sign, this leads you into a green hedged path. This path between the field edges continues till the bushes give way to crops. Turn left by the waymarks; you are now 40 feet from the road. Head left for the footpath sign half hidden in the tree at the roadside.

❾ On reaching the road turn right and walk for some ½ mile till you see the RAF memorial. In summer the combination of the dark red roses and the poignant words remembering 121 members of the Allied Air Forces who left this airfield will tug at your heart.

⑩ Take care on the busy road. You continue, passing two brick cottages on your left, then go left onto the road that passes Down Hall Lodge. Ignore the right turning ahead. You may glimpse the church tower in the trees. On entering the village you pass interesting cottages that lead round the corner to the post office shop. Finish the walk by going left through the churchyard to your car.

WEST MERSEA

Length: 6¼ miles

Getting there: From the south via Maldon, then on the B1026 to Salcott. Follow the signs through Gt Wigborough and Peldon to Mersea Island. From east, west and north, find your	way to Colchester then take the B1025 south to the island. **Parking:** Follow the signs for West Mersea till you come to High Street. Turn right into the	public car park with toilets right beside the library. **Map:** OS Landranger – Colchester and the Blackwater 168 (GR 009125).

West Mersea has a very long history. The Romans built a 65 foot watch tower here to help guard access to the Blackwater. Not surprisingly, many Roman artefacts have been unearthed in the area, including pieces from mosaic floors. On one occasion, on a farm about a mile out of

town excavators found a small tiled chamber. Inside was a lead casket containing a bowl of pale green glass, the last resting place of a Roman cremated in the first century. The site can be glimpsed in the distance on the walk from Dawes Road. Mersea has seen other invaders too.

FOOD and DRINK

There is a wide range of food available from the cafe, the restaurant and White Hart pub all near the car park. There is also a fish and chip shop, a delicatessen and Arthur Cook the butcher if you need to take home supplies.

In AD 895 the Danes tried to launch an attack on London from here.

Mersea has become a popular holiday island, sometimes cut off from the mainland at the Strood, the Roman causeway, at times of high tides. In February 1953 part of the area was affected by the great storm that flooded the coastline from Harwich to East London. Both sailors and those intent on a good picnic and a family fun day out will find plenty to interest them here. In the small area around West Mersea church you will find a wide range of shops and eating places.

Just down the hill from the car park you come to the beach. Following this lovely route you will walk along the shore enjoying the sea breezes, and then climb up the hill to get better views of the island.

THE WALK

❶ Leave the car park and at the library turn right downhill till you come to Garden Cottage. Cross the road and head for the footpath sign. Go down the steps to the beach.

❷ Turn left and make your way along about 2 miles of coastline. Across the Blackwater you have good views of Bradwell. On your left as you walk you will pass Two Sugars Cafe, several toilet blocks,

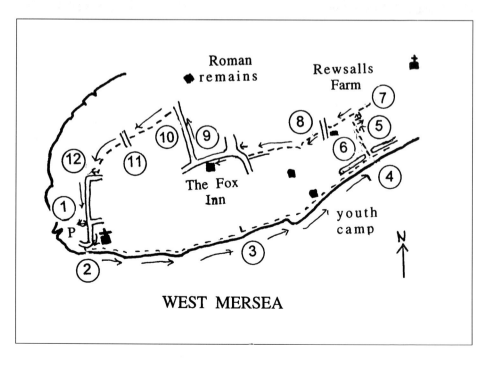

WEST MERSEA

The beach at West Mersea.

Country Fare, and rows of beach huts. Near the end of the huts, at the very high tide mark, aim for the squeeze gate ahead.

❸ Ignore the path off left and continue round Waldegraves Caravan Park and Mersea Youth Camp. There is a fine sea wall here. Cross the stile.

❹ Immediately after the second stile turn left downhill through a wire fence and head inland on an earth bridge between two dikes to a stile. Keep straight on with the hedge on your right.

❺ At the end of the first field turn right through a metal farm gate, then immediately left to the corner of this field where there is a stile in a reeded area.

❻ Over the stile turn right and follow the field edge round and uphill. As the field edge turns right you should continue across the cultivated field. It is a shame the farmer does not reinstate this path. When you reach a hollow with some trees turn right. Walk along the field edge. When you come to the end turn left and walk uphill. If the cultivated field is impassable do as the locals do and follow the original field edge right to the hedge line and climb this till you reach ❼.

❼ As you nearly reach the top of the contour line your way is crossed by a track. This is where you turn left and walk

---

PLACES of INTEREST

The **Mersea Island Museum** is in the High Street, open May to September, Wednesday to Sunday afternoons. It has many items of local interest and stages special exhibitions (telephone: 01206 385191). **Cudmore Grove Country Park** at East Mersea is ideal for a picnic, open daily (telephone: 01206 383868).

---

towards Rewsalls Farm. The track brings you out onto the farm road.

❽ Turn right, then left across the road. At the footpath sign continue walking west on another firm track. Ignore the bridge on the right and continue on the track till you come to the road and a footpath sign. Cross this road with care as it is busy in the summer time and continue to walk in the same direction to a T-junction.

❾ Turn left. The Fox Inn is about 300 yards on the left, a good place to stop if you are thirsty. Continue for another 200 yards and turn right up Dawes Lane.

❿ After ½ mile look at about one o'clock. There is the mound where the Roman remains were found. Turn left at the footpath sign and cross the field on a well defined path passing the rear of the farm on the way to the road.

⓫ At the signpost opposite continue ahead on a concrete track that becomes a cross-field path and then out to the road at the footpath sign.

⓬ Turn right and after a few yards left into High Street North. Walk down this and into High Street to get back to your car.

WIVENHOE

Length: 5 miles

Getting there: Wivenhoe is situated on the river Colne between Clacton and Colchester. From Colchester take the A133 toward Clacton. Just past University of Essex buildings take the B1027 Clacton road and after ½ mile keep right on to the	B1028. Ignore two further left turns as you go downhill into Wivenhoe village centre. **Parking:** Either on the road outside the church or if this is full in the public car park in Clifton Terrace (just opposite the Grey-	hound pub). There are public toilets here. **Map:** OS Landranger – Colchester and the Blackwater 168 (GR 039216 car park, 039214 church).

This proud old-fashioned village is built on a hill, rising from the quay on the river Colne. It also faces the Roman river. The buildings in the High Street are interesting and date back 300 years, over a time when ship-building and the farming of oysters were important industries. Much of the church was rebuilt after the 1884 earthquake that caused damage in many parts of Essex.

There is so much to see on this walk. You will wander along the quay, passing

FOOD and DRINK

There are several good pubs in the town but we chose the Rose and Crown down on the quay. It is a sun trap for those wishing to sit outdoors. Their menu includes a range of ploughman's, baguettes, open sandwiches and hot sandwiches. We chose their rare roast beef open sandwiches and thoroughly enjoyed them. There is very limited car parking at the pub so I would recommend you leave your car and walk down for your refreshments.

the Nottage Institute, a Royal Yachting Association's shorebased establishment which offers tuition and also houses a museum of local history and marine heritage. The route then takes you along the river bank through an interesting mix of houses and gardens to pass the new Colne Barrier before heading into more remote, open land. There are many good picnic spots along the river bank for those wishing to take their own food with them.

There are no visible remains of the Roman villa near Alresford Lodge, but the ridge walk back into the village is superb. It gives wide views over several large lakes, north to the old ruined church and south to the Fingringhoe Nature Reserve on the other bank of the Colne.

THE WALK

❶ From the car park walk downhill past the church to the quay. Turn left to pass the Nottage Institute and walk along the river front till you join The Folley. Go slightly

The quay.

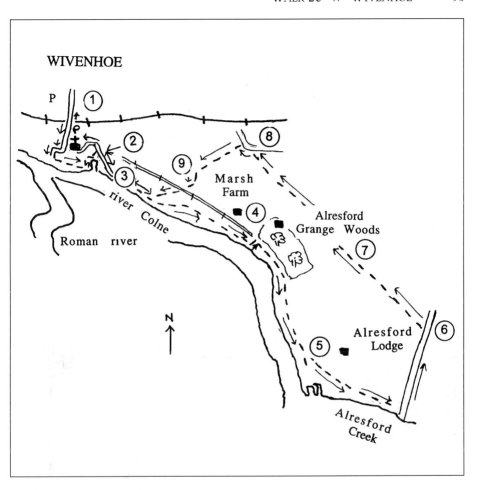

WIVENHOE

left and walk up this right of way between houses and gardens.

❷ A black and yellow direction post guides you round the rear of a dock then inland to the road. At the road there are two direction posts, so turn right and make your way up to the Colne Barrier.

❸ Walk past the barrier buildings and in front of Wivenhoe sailing club. You will find yourself on a good gravel path on the river bank that leads you through a kissing gate. Follow this path, ignoring a path off to your left. Pass a bench, then a second bench and stile. The old railway line with Marsh Farm behind can clearly be seen on your left as you approach a seat.

❹ You now walk slightly left and then right through Alresford Grange Woods. Ignore the private gate and also the footpath sign indicating a path joining on your left.

❺ As you pass Alresford Lodge the path divides and you need to go leftish between two heavy concrete posts. Walk on with a wire fence on your left. The path quickly becomes hedged on both sides as you approach the gravel works. Walk under the old line of the gravel works rigging – how long ago, one wonders, was it when the last shipment of gravel left the site using this route?

❻ On reaching the road and direction post, turn left and walk uphill. Ignore the footpath off to the right half-way up the hill. As you approach the gravel works be aware large lorries can appear along the next 400 yards of the walk so take care. At the crest of the hill turn left at a public bridleway sign. The track is marked 'Private Road to Creek Lodge and Alresford Lodge'. The bridleway runs on the left of the concrete quarry road.

❼ Pass the AAA private car park and the right turn off to the ruined church. Watch for crossing quarry vehicles as you cross a track to enter an old road to the left of the new concrete quarry road. Walk on to pass a gatehouse and follow the old road till you come to the bridleway sign and the road.

❽ Turn left along this rather busy road.

PLACES of INTEREST

Colchester has something for everyone with its castle, museums, craft centre, zoo, and country park. Telephone the Tourist Information Centre on 01206 282828, for further information.

There is a grass verge on the right-hand side if you prefer to cross to this. When you come to The Chase turn left at the black and yellow footpath post and cross the stile. The path lies ahead between two fences. As you descend you get good views over the Colne Valley. You come to some very low branches just before the next stile. Go over this and take the path ahead through an open area to the old railway line.

❾ Cross the railway line and go over the stile ahead. The path takes you back to the Colne and the way you know, back to your car. Take this if you wish to return to the quay for a drink. If you are heading straight back to town continue on this road till you come to the T-junction by Wivenhoe Business Centre. Turn left and follow the road round. Go straight across at the junction and then immediately right through a metal church gate into the rear of the churchyard. From here you walk through to the High Street and your car.